DAVID IRVING

The Night the
Dams Burst

David Irving is the son of a Royal Navy commander.

After visiting Imperial College of Science & Technology and University College London, he spent a year in the Ruhr, Germany, working in a steel mill and perfecting his fluency in the German language.

Among his thirty-odd books, the best-known include Hitler's War; Churchill's War, vol i: "Struggle for Power," vol. ii: "Triumph in Adversity", and vol. iii: "The Sundered Dream"; Accident, the Death of General Sikorski; The Destruction of Dresden; The Mare's Nest; The German Atomic Bomb; The Destruction of Convoy PQ17; The Rise and Fall of the Luftwaffe; The Trail of the Fox: the Search for the True Field Marshal Rommel; Hess, the Missing Years, and Nuremberg, the Last Battle.

He has also translated several works by other authors including Field-Marshal Wilhelm Keitel, Reinhard Gehlen, and Nikki Lauda. He lives in Windsor, England, and has raised five daughters.

DAVID IRVING

The Night the Dams Burst

[**REAL** HEROISM
[**REAL** ADVENTURE
[**REAL HISTORY**

F
FOCAL POINT

Focal Point Classic Edition ISBN 1–872197–3–5

Based on three articles by the author first published in The
Sunday Express, London, in May 1973. We acknowledge
Crown copyright in some documents and photographs used.
Every effort has been made to trace copyright holders of
other images, and they are invited to contact us at info@fpp.
co.uk

Readers are invited to report any typographical errors
to David Irving by email at info@fpp.co.uk. Informed
comments and corrections on historical points are also
welcomed.

Printed in the United States of America
Focal Point Publications
Windsor SL4 6QS
England

A SPECIAL FOUR-PART HISTORY of the heroic RAF Bomber Command attack on the Ruhr Dams in May 1943, immortalised by the British movie *The Dambusters*. David Irving wrote the original account for *The Sunday Express*, London, in May 1973. He used official British and German documents, and interviews with the surviving airmen and with Barnes Wallis, the British scientist who invented the unique "bouncing bomb" which smashed the dams. Wallis gave him exclusive access to his private papers and diaries. The author has expanded his account with materials which have become available since then.

Books by David Irving

Und Deutschlands Städte Starben Nicht (*with Günter Karweina*)
The Destruction of Dresden
The Mare's Nest
The Destruction of Convoy PQ.17
The Memoirs of Field Marshal Keitel (*translator*)
Accident. The Death of General Sikorski
The Virus House
Formula 1: The Art & Science of Grand Prix Driving, by Niki Lauda (translator)
Breach of Security (*with Prof. D C Watt*)
The Service. The Memoirs of General Reinhard Gehlen (*translator and editor*)
The Rise and Fall of the Luftwaffe
Hitler und seine Feldherren
Hitler's War
The Trail of the Fox
The War Path
Der Nürnberger Prozess
Mord aus Staatsräson
Wie Krank War Hitler Wirklich ?
Uprising! One Nation's Nightmare: Hungary 1956
The War between the Generals
Von Guernica bis Vietnam
The Secret Diaries of Hitler's Doctor
Adolf Hitler: The Medical Diaries
Der Morgenthau-Plan 1944/45 (*documentation*)
Churchill's War vol. i: "The Struggle for Power"
Göring. A Biography
Hess: The Missing Years
Führer und Reichskanzler
Das Reich hört mit
Deutschlands Ostgrenze
Hitler's War & The War Path (*updated, one-volume edition*)
Die Nacht, in der die Dämme Brachen
Der unbekannte Dr. Goebbels (1938 *diary transcribed*)
Apocalypse 1945. The Destruction of Dresden
Goebbels. Mastermind of the Third Reich
Nuremberg, the Last Battle
"Churchill's War", vol. ii: "Triumph in Adversity"
Banged Up: Survival as a Political Prisoner in 21st Century Europe

IN PREPARATION:
"Churchill's War", vol. iii: "The Sundered Dream"
Heinrich Himmler

The Night the Dams Burst

by David Irving

CHAPTER ONE: In which Mr Barnes Wallis fights for acceptance of his revolutionary new weapon. then sees it fail   *Page 9*

CHAPTER TWO: In which Mr Barnes Wallis gets the special bomb to work, and the raid begins   *Page 47*

CHAPTER THREE: In which the Ruhr Dams are breached   *Page 85*

Afterword: It was the back spin that did the trick   *Page 116*

Notes and Sources   Page 134

One of Britain's great commanders, Marshal of the Royal Air Force Sir Arthur Harris: above with US air force general Ira Eaker two months after the Dams Raid in 1943; below with author David Irving in 1962.

CHAPTER ONE: In which Mr Barnes Wallis fights for acceptance of his revolutionary new weapon but then sees it fail

"THIRTY-NINE MILE AN HOUR, I makes it," said the plain-clothes policeman. He opened his notebook and solemnly eyed the watch in his hand.

White-haired and timid, the driver of the small black Wolseley Ten saloon blinked at him absently from behind metal-rimmed spectacles.

"By Jove, was I really doing that, officer? My mind must have been miles away."

Mr Barnes Wallis looked at his own watch. He was anxious: it was half-past eleven, and at noon he had to be at the Vickers building in Westminster. But here he was, still in Putney Vale.

"I am on urgent business, officer – Government business. It's top secret," he stammered.

The policeman grunted, unimpressed. "Really?" he said, licked his thumb, and turned over a new page in his notebook.

Wallis groaned. He knew that he was carrying a top-secret film and that he should have an armed RAF guard with him. But this morning the instructions to report to London had come too suddenly for that.

Just two hours before, Sir Charles Craven, the Chairman and Managing Director of Vickers-Armstrong, had telephoned him at his drawing-office near Weybridge, and ordered him to come up to town at once: "The First Sea Lord wants to see your film of 'Highball'," he said. "The one you dropped at Chesil Beach."

To cap it all, just as he had been leaving the Vickers Works, the works foreman had run out and told him that a crack had been found in a Wellington bomber's spar, and it needed an urgent decision. Barnes Wallis was the famous aircraft's designer. That had delayed him for a good half hour. And now this.

"Can I see your driving licence, Sir?"

Wallis fumed. He was deceptively mild-mannered, slight in build, and with innocent grey-blue eyes behind those metal frames. Keeping their Lordships of the Admiralty waiting was one thing, but he dreaded the wrath of Sir Charles: Commander Sir Charles Worthington Craven was a powerful man, and Barnes Wallis had more than once fallen foul of him in his long career.

He was nearly half an hour late when he finally stumbled into the private cinema in the Vickers company's headquarters building in Westminster, clutching the precious reel of film under one arm. Four or five admirals were standing around, shifting from one foot to another in extreme impatience. Admiral Sir Dudley Pound, the First Sea Lord, was talking to Craven, and Wallis could see that the glowering Vickers chairman was not in a benign mood towards aircraft engineers today.

What saved Wallis from Sir Charles now was the amazing film he had brought with him.

Onto the screen flickered a title: "Most Secret Trial Number One." Then the camera's telescopic lens focused onto the dark shape of a Wellington bomber, flying low over the waves just off shore.

"That is Chesil Beach," said Barnes Wallis. "Now — watch that bulge hanging beneath the plane ... "

The bulge was a large black ball, about four feet six inches in diameter. It was obviously spinning backwards at high speed. A light flashed in the cockpit, and the steel ball dropped towards the sea.

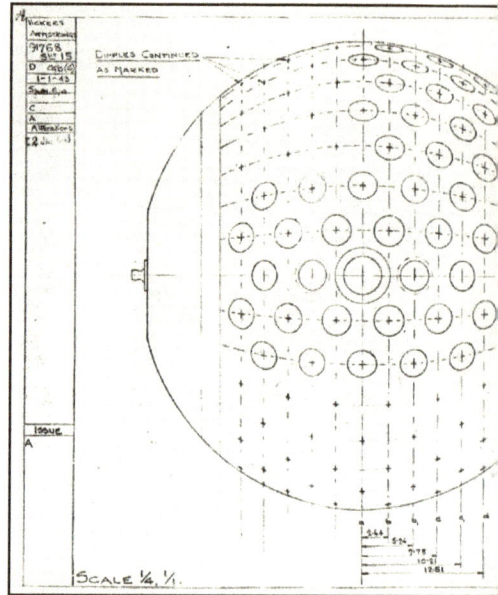

That was when the surprises began. Not only did this strange heavy ball fall much more slowly than seemed normal, but when it struck the sea it bounced – it bounced not once but twelve, then thirteen times, with Wallis jubilantly counting each bounce out aloud. It had bounded about half a mile along the sea's surface before it finally ploughed into a wave and sank.

"That's it!" announced Wallis. "That bomb answers most of the problems facing the Air Force today. Dropped at high altitude over Germany, it will float down much

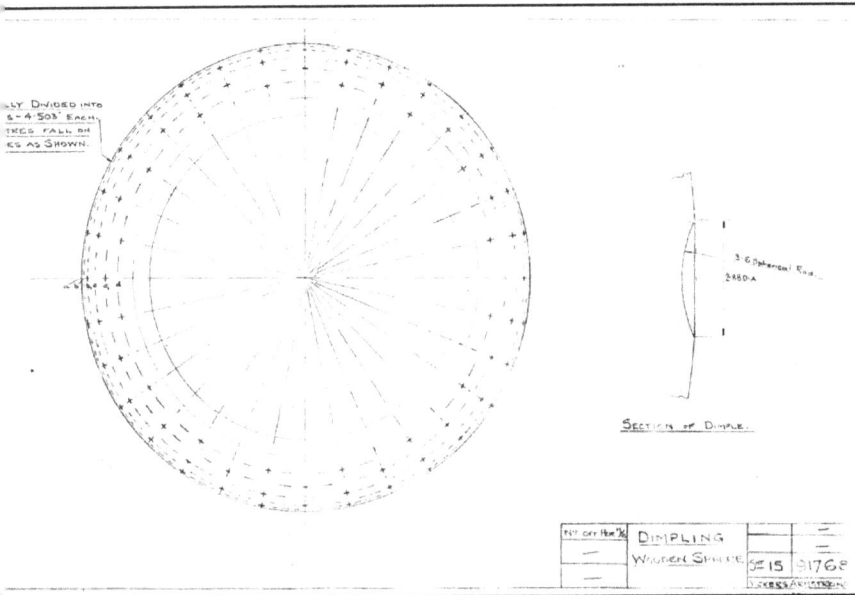

Wallis originally designed his bomb as a sphere. Testing was carried out from December 1942 at Chesil in Dorset. It proved prone to impact damage. Vickers produced this wooden version, dimpled like a golf ball. First tested on Saturday January 23, 1943 the wooden sphere bounced thirteen times.

more slowly – so it can be dropped from further outside the range of specially defended targets. Used as a naval weapon, it will bounce over any of the booms and torpedo nets that the enemy uses to protect his warships at anchor – and his huge dams."

He chuckled, like a conjurer who has just pulled off a particularly pleasing trick. "And," he said, "when it strikes a battleship's side, because of its back-spin, it will actually curve inwards beneath the ship's hull as it sinks – so it can be exploded just where the enemy has never bothered to put any armourplate."

SINKING BATTLESHIPS alone would not win the war. Wallis believed however that there was one operation that just might do that: he had been fighting for years for one massive attack to be carried out on Germany's most vital dams – a project he had dubbed "An Engineer's Way to Win the War."

This was typical Barnes Wallis. He was outstandingly capable of thinking up new ideas – almost all of which met with fierce opposition from officialdom: he probably preferred it that way. When Professor Sir Thomas Merton, one of Winston Churchill's leading scientists, had first been approached by Wallis with the Dambusting bomb idea, his first feeling was, This man's absolutely cracked. But, he later told the author, "after Wallis had been there for half an hour, I realised that I was talking to one of the greatest engineering geniuses of the world's history."

Much of Wallis's wartime genius had been applied to ball-shaped things. Once he had written to a newspaper that he could design a cricket ball which would put both sides "out" twice in a day, and would be indistinguishable from a standard ball. The Cricket Club secretaries had persuaded him in anguish not to proceed with the idea.

What Wallis had in mind for the four-ton ball he called "Upkeep" was not cricket.

"There are five dams in the Ruhr, gentlemen," he told the admirals. "Without them, Germany's power-stations can't make steam, her canals will either overflow or run dry and her most vital factories will be devastated by flooding. One dam, in particular, regulates the supply of the only sulphur-free water available to the Ruhr's steel-works. Do you know, it takes over 100 tons of water to make one ton of steel? This dam, the Möhne Dam, holds back 134,000,000 tons of water. . ."

He continued enthusiastically, "My staff and I have shown – we have tried it out on model dams – that even with a charge as small as 6,500 pounds of RDX explosive, we can destroy the Möhne Dam, the biggest of the five, provided that the explosion occurs in actual contact with the masonry.

"My bouncing bomb will do just that. Just as the naval

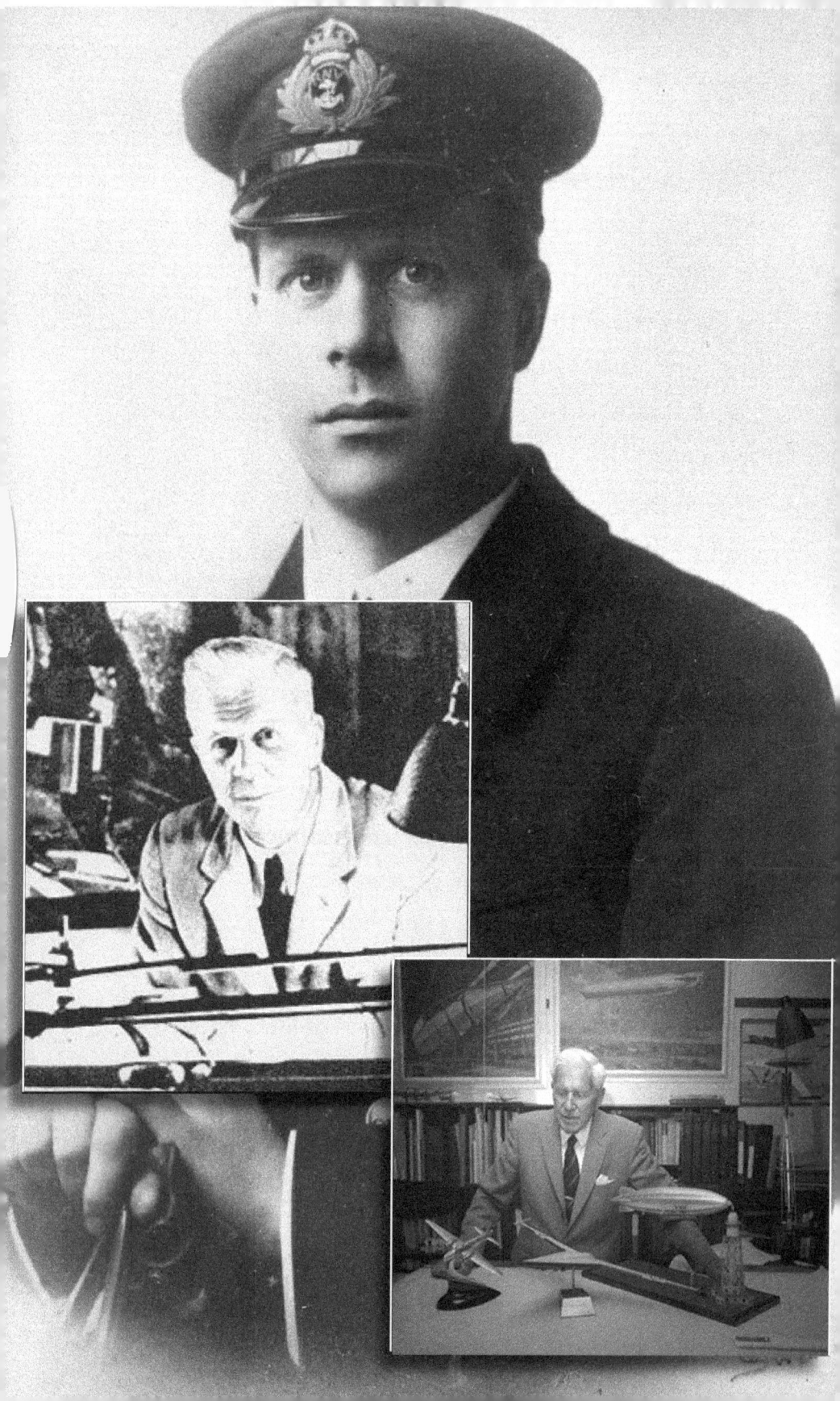

Six weeks before the raid, No. 541 Squadron brought back reconnaissance photos of the Möhne Dam

LEFT: *A snotty (sublieutenant) in World War I, Barnes Wallis was a brilliant aircraft designer in World War II and on into the space age*

version will curve underneath the enemy's warship, so the dam-busting weapon, over seven times as heavy, will curve in towards the dam-wall as it sinks and cling to it all the way down until the charge goes off."

The admirals had not come to listen to talk of attacking dams – they wanted to sink the German Navy, and in particular the battleship *Tirpitz*. If Wallis's theory was right, the bomb need be no bigger than could fit snugly into the twin-engined Mosquito bomber's bomb bay. This was just what they needed.

After the film show, Air Marshal John Linnell, the Controller of Research and Development at the Ministry of Aircraft Production – and one of Wallis's most determined opponents – grudgingly agreed to lend him two of the precious Mosquitoes for trials of the anti-*Tirpitz* bomb. Furthermore, at ten o'clock on the following morning, the local boss of Vickers, Major Kilner, rang Wallis breathlessly from London: "The Admiralty have given us the go-ahead! Two hundred and fifty of the 'Highball' bombs are to be put in hand – top priority – at once."

WALLIS WAS NOT OVERJOYED. It was good news, but still only a very low rung on a tall ladder. Sinking battleships would not win wars in the way that the sudden destruction of all Germany's most important dams might.

As he put the phone down, Wallis also realised that once the weapon had been used against the *Tirpitz*, all hope of surprise in using it against the dams would be lost. He had to bring immediate and equal priority to the attack on the dams, and the only way to do that was to get the Prime Minister interested.

This in turn would mean winning Lord Cherwell, the physicist and politician who exploited his friendship with Mr Churchill to devastating effect, for the cause.

Superficially, Cherwell and Barnes Wallis were similar: both shunned drink and tobacco, and both were extreme vegetarians. But there the similarity ended. The Prof., as Cherwell was known in Churchill's intimate circle, was ruthless in manner and Central European in aspect; Barnes Wallis was the typical English country parson's son – self-effacing and slight. Above all, Cherwell was an eminent theoretical scientist, whose career had begun in the universities of Darmstadt and Berlin, while Wallis was an engineer who had started humbly as an apprentice in a shipyard at a wage of four shillings per week.

All in all, Wallis did not rate his chances of interesting

Winston Churchill too highly. He had had a discouraging experience with Cherwell – then still Professor Lindemann – in 1940, and the last time he had called to see him he had been left waiting in an ante-room for two hours while numbers of young men wafted in and out and assured him that "their Prof." would be back from lunch any moment now. On that occasion, Cherwell had crushed him with the words, "You know, Mr Wallis, we don't think these dams are very interesting as targets."

Perhaps Wallis did not know it, but the hostility was not personally directed against him, but another product of the now famous behind-the-scenes Whitehall feud between Cherwell and Sir Henry Tizard, whose position as senior scientific advisor the Prof had usurped.

Tizard had backed the Dams Bomb project all along, and made no secret of it; he had promoted it in letters to the ministries, and to Mr Churchill himself. Above all, it was Tizard who had obtained for Wallis permission from the National Physical Laboratory at Teddington to carry out a series of spectacular model-scale experiments with two-inch steel balls catapulted down the length of the laboratory's experimental model-ship tank.

This time, Wallis would not repeat his 1940 mistake.

He wrote Lord Cherwell a letter. With the letter he sent a twenty-page report, marked secret, and complete with photographs and diagrams; working from facts provided by an officer of the Secret Service, he proved beyond doubt the importance of the five major Ruhr Dams, and explained the whole theory of the spinning bomb – its aerodynamic and hydrodynamic effects.

Wallis had even found proof of the invention two centuries earlier of a gun able to fire round corners, using the same principle; the intrepid eighteenth-century inventor had demonstrated his weapon before an audience at the Royal Society, a body of which Lord Cherwell was now himself a prominent member.

"Unfortunately," explained Barnes Wallis in his letter to the professor, "the possibilities of this new weapon [the spinning bomb] against naval targets appear to have overshadowed the question of the destruction of the major German dams." If the consequent delay in developing the four-ton dambusting weapon known as "Upkeep" lasted any longer, he said, the whole plan would have to be shelved for a year.

"Large-scale experiments carried out against similar dams in Wales have shown that it is possible to destroy the German dams if the attack is made at a time when these are full of water." In practice that would mean May – mid-May, since the moon would also have to be full. It was now already the end of January 1943.

His present orders were to develop within the next six weeks the anti-*Tirpitz* bomb, "Highball," for the Mosquito. Given equal priority, he promised that he could do a similar job on the Dams Bomb for the Lancaster Bomber: "Two months," was the promise that he made in his letter.

Two days later, on February 2, 1943, he followed the letter up with a personal visit to Lord Cherwell and showed him the film of the Wellington bomber trials two weeks before.

With sinking heart, he watched Lord Cherwell's face: no spark of enthusiasm could be seen. In fact, among the papers of the late Lord Cherwell which this author has reviewed, there is no indication that Churchill's scientific adviser took any action whatsoever after Wallis's visit.

FOR A WHILE the "Upkeep" bomb project stagnated.

Wallis was moving in a jungle peopled by opponents and apathetic civil servants; frequently it was impossible to tell the one from the other. David Pye, the Director of Scientific Research at the Air Ministry and also chairman of a committee that had been set up in 1940 to study the possibilities of attacking the German dams, was one of the shrewdest of Wallis's opponents – always seeming to help, without quite doing so. Later on the same day as Wallis's visit to Lord Cherwell, he was with Pye.

Pye said: "You've got our authority to proceed with design work for the installations of the bomb and its gear in the Lancaster." Wallis, with long experience of civil service methods, demanded: "Can I have that confirmed in writing? And I shall need a full set of the Lancaster's drawings sent down to me . . . "

"Ah, that's a different matter," snorted Pye. "The Lancaster's one of our most secret planes, and the blueprints are not being shown to anybody."

Wallis sighed. He would have to pull still more strings – and he was running out of them. Besides, he needed the bombers themselves, not just the blueprints. Within a few days, all that he had been given was the vague promise of the loan of a Lancaster, but on February 19, 1943 bureaucracy dealt him another blow.

Air Marshall Linnell telephoned him, and with a clear

note of triumph in his voice ordered him to stop work on the Dams Bomb.

It had been decided that there was to be no further action on it. Wallis again felt himself without friends. Dr Baker, the elderly superintendent of the ship tank at Teddington laboratory, mercilessly told him, "Stop playing the fool and go and do something useful for the war . . ."

That evening, Wallis had a private call from Flight Lieutenant Green, his liaison officer to the Ministry of Aircraft Production. Green confirmed his fears. In his diary, Wallis wrote: "Green says that DSR [David Pye] having ensured CRD's [Air Marshal Linnell's] refusal now pretends to back the scheme."

A few days later, injury was added to insult: a brown paper envelope arrived, and Wallis learned that he had been fined two pounds for the speeding offence in Putney Vale, despite a plea by the security service to the magistrate, that Wallis was working on the most urgent Government business.

*

Wallis swallowed his pride, and asked Dr Baker to let him prepare one final experiment in the lab's busy ship-testing tank. It would have to be an experiment capable of making even the most hard-boiled civil servant sit up and take notice.

He built a model dam across the water tank, and catapulted the two-inch balls at it. A girl cinematographer submerged in an airtight glass tank filmed the spinning spheres as they struck the dam and sank. Wallis showed the film to the Air Staff – there were audible gasps as the submerged camera showed the spinning balls "cling" to the model dam's face as they sank.

There were louder gasps when Wallis showed them and some admirals an even more spectacular experiment in the tank at Teddington: he had moored a large model ship across the tank to represent the *Tirpitz*. On a signal from him, the assistant fired the first two-inch steel ball. It streaked down the tank, struck the model ship and sank, still spinning, out of sight – to reappear suddenly on the other side of the battleship, having passed right beneath the model's hull.

"I think I have made my point," said Wallis quietly.

He was able to show film of this experiment to Sir Charles Portal and the First Sea Lord on February 19. Portal was now willing for the RAF to begin planning an attack on the dams, but he could imagine what Bomber Command's reaction was likely to be.

In fact, he had discovered that Air Chief Marshal Sir Arthur Harris – "Butcher" Harris – was hostile to any idea of a dambusting operation. Harris needed every Lancaster he could get for more urgent assignments over Germany, with conventional and trusted weapons like blockbusters and incendiaries. He had run into inventors who thought they had a simple way to win the war before.

As Portal watched the film with Barnes Wallis he thought of the letter he had received that morning from Harris. In this, Harris – whose Intelligence "grapevine" was evidently operating at high efficiency – complained, "All sorts of enthusiasts and panacea-mongers are careering round the Ministry of Aircraft Production suggesting that about thirty Lancasters should be taken off the line and modified to carry a new and revolutionary bomb, which exists only in the imagination of those who conceived it. . . "

Strictly speaking, that much was true, of course. Barnes Wallis had not yet built, let alone tested, a full-size "Upkeep" rotating bomb. After seeing Wallis's amazing new film, the Chief of Air Staff wrote back to Harris. "I will not allow," Portal promised, "more than three of your precious Lancasters to be diverted."

Before he got more, Wallis would have to show that his bomb worked in the full scale. To Wallis, in the meantime, Portal heartlessly offered no words of encouragement at all.

Wallis, independently, decided to tackle Harris, the awesome bomber commander, himself. He telephoned his chief test pilot, "Mutt" Summers.

"Mutt," he said, "we'll have to find some way of showing this film to 'Butch' Harris. You know him personally, don't you?"

"Sure, we were in the Royal Flying Corps together."

Summers rang up Harris's deputy, Air Vice-Marshal Sir Robert Saundby. A trip to the RAF Bomber Command headquarters outside High Wycombe was arranged.

Once more Wallis stowed his precious films into the back of his Wolseley, and this time he sat "Mutt" Summers in the front. Together they drove to High Wycombe on the afternoon of February 22.

As he was shown into Harris's office the air chief marshal glowered. "Now what the hell is it that you want?"

he rasped. "I won't have you damned inventors wasting all my time!"

Barnes Wallis was unaware of Harris's unflattering remarks about him in his letter to Portal. But Harris's aversion to all inventors was understandable. As a fighter pilot at Northolt outside London in the First World War, he had been plagued by them and any one of them might willingly have been his downfall.

Several legends surrounded this. One inventor had shown him a grapnel, and proposed that Harris should sling it out at the Zeppelin airships wreaking havoc in English towns at that time. Harris had bluntly replied, "My aircraft's horsepower is 80, the Zeppelin's is 1600. Before I start hooking my plane onto a Zepp, I shall want to know who is going home with whom!"

Undeterred, that inventor had reappeared at Harris's airfield with the thing in a suitcase, which he set down on the ground. He said, "I've got it now," he said. "I've put a small explosive charge on it. All you do is press this" – and the rest of the sentence was abbreviated by a shattering roar as the suitcase blew up of its own accord.

"I HAVE AN IDEA for a bomb," began Barnes Wallis

now, blinking short-sightedly at Harris and groping for his spectacles. "A bomb which will destroy the Möhne Dam."

Harris groaned silently. "I've heard about it," he said. "It's far-fetched."

Wallis mentally noted that Harris had been "very much misinformed re job" (as he put it in his diary).

He launched into a long technical explanation of the principle of the spectacular weapon and concluded: ". . . You see, if the bomb has a back spin on it, it will be forced against the dam face all the time it is sinking, and it will explode in contact, just as we require."

Harris was taking more notice now. There was something about this quiet-spoken engineer that separated him from the rest. In any case, the genius who had designed the sturdy Wellesley and Wellington bombers could not be ignored. Nodding at the projectionist threading the film into the machine, Harris grunted to Wallis: "If this thing's as good as you say, the fewer people who know about it the better." He turned to his deputy. "Saundby, you work the projector."

In the headquarters cinema, with nobody watching except the two air marshals, Wallis, and his test pilot, the top secret films of the underwater antics of the rotating bomb "Upkeep" and the airborne trials of "Highball" off Chesil Beach were shown again. No sound was heard except the whirring of the projector. When the lights came on again, Harris's pink-complexioned, puffy face was expressionless. He tossed a letter to Wallis, and said, "You'd better read this."

It was the letter from Sir Portal, requiring Harris to lend three Lancasters to Wallis for the full-scale "Upkeep" trials.

Wallis had no idea of how well he had scored personally with Harris. He could not penetrate the mask of the air marshal's face. As they left, he took Summers' arm and said in relief, "Well, that wasn't too bad after all, was it!"

In fact his troubles were not over. Harris – impressed though he was – still refused to withdraw a Lancaster squadron from the front line to train for the dams attack. And at this moment, another force intervened with Wallis – almost certainly guided by the hand of the short-sighted Air Marshal Linnell, who had blocked "Upkeep" at every stage.

At ten a.m. on the morning after his face-to-face meeting with Harris, he and "Mutt" Summers were ordered to report to Major Kilner's office at the Vickers works. Kilner unhappily told them that Sir Charles Craven, Vickers's chief executive, had ordered them both to London at once.

At Vickers House, the air was frigid with hostility. "I have been asked to tell you," Craven snapped at Wallis, "that you are to stop your nonsense about destroying dams. I have been officially advised that Mr Wallis of Vickers is making a damn' nuisance of himself. You are wasting the Government's and the firm's time and money – you are to start working on something useful for once. You are forbidden to work any longer on this absurd bouncing-bomb project."

In a final grotesque outburst, he shouted hysterically at Wallis. "And what happened on the Golf Links at Ulverston?"

To Wallis, the whole row was beyond comprehension, let alone Craven's final cryptic challenge. The slight white-haired engineer looked the powerfully built former naval commander in the eye and said, "Well, Sir, if I'm not serving the best interests of the company and the country, I had better offer you my resignation."

It was coolly said; it was meant; and it was too much.

Like Captain Bligh of the *Bounty*, Sir Charles Craven stood up, and crashed his fist down onto the desk, bellowing, "Mutiny, mutiny, mutiny!"

Barnes Wallis stalked sorrowfully out. In his diary he wrote: "Private interview afterwards with [Major] Kilner, and told him again [am] anxious to go . . . "

He lunched at the RAF Club in Piccadilly with the Secret Service officer who had given him such support before, and both recognised that their only hope now was Mr Churchill.

*

The way through Lord Cherwell was evidently barred. But Mr Churchill was also known to rely extensively on a scientific committee set up earlier in the war by Mr Oliver Lyttelton, and it was to two of this committee's three members, Sir Sydney Barratt and Professor Merton, that Wallis went, in Richmond Terrace, that afternoon, still shaken by the mauling meted out to him by Craven.

The two scientists could see that something out of the ordinary had happened.

Wallis answered their questioning looks: "I'm done

for," he murmured. "I've resigned from Vickers. The dams plan is off." Barratt, who would later become chairman of the mighty Albright & Wilson chemicals concern, questioned Wallis for ninety minutes on the scientific basis of the case, and then Wallis left for home.

This meeting proved to be the turning point, Mr Churchill called for the papers on "Upkeep" and then, his imagination fired, gave the order for the dams raid to be prepared on top priority. At three o'clock on the afternoon of February 26, Barnes Wallis's hour of sweet revenge arrived, when he and Craven were summoned to the room of his old enemy, Air Marshal Linnell.

Evidently controlling himself with some difficulty, Linnell informed Wallis that the War Cabinet had directed that the development and testing of the dambusting bomb, and the modified Lancaster bombers that were to carry it, were to proceed at once. Choking with rage, he told Wallis: "The Air Staff have ordered me that you are to be given everything you want." A few days later, Linnell announced his intention of resigning.

To say that "Bomber" Harris remained privately unconvinced would be wrong: In fact, he was outraged. He continued to deprecate any diversion of his precious new Lancasters from Bomber Command's main task of pulverising Germany's cities.

After Saundby first told him of Wallis's proposals, Harris wrote an acid denunciation of the scheme in February 1943. He protested to the Air Staff that the bouncing bomb was tripe beyond the wildest description: "There are so many ifs and buts," he wrote, "that there is not the smallest chance of it working." He pleaded with them not to put any of their new Lancasters aside "on this wild goose chase," as this would only dilute his saturation bombing campaign. He predicted that the war would be over before the Wallis bomb ever worked, adding, "and it never will."

A few days later he described the weapon to his superior, Sir Charles Portal, as "just about the maddest proposition we have yet to come across." He was prepared to bet his shirt, he added, that the bomb could not be produced within six months, and "will not work when we have got it."

Yes, Harris was a bluff commander, one of Britain's greatest, and he did not mince his language. He proposed to the Air Staff that they give Wallis and his enthusiasts "one aeroplane to go away and play, while we get on with the war." It was one battle that Harris lost.

Portal overruled him, and Harris had to obey.

The Air Staff now formed a new Lancaster squadron, No. 617, under the command of Guy Gibson, a particularly experienced pilot. Eventually it would adopt a famous motto: *Après moi de déluge.*

MANY YEARS AFTERWARDS Wallis would explain: "Half the joy in life really consists in the fight, not in the subsequent success."

Now his fight against bureaucracy was suddenly and unexpectedly over – but the result of the long delays was that he had now only eight weeks left to do the job. As he left Linnell's room, he felt physically sick, and lonelier than ever before in his life. They've called my bluff, he thought. And out loud he said, "If only I had somebody to lean on. . ."

The Director of Technical Development, Norbert Rowe, must have overheard him, for next morning there was a letter in the post at Wallis's drawing office: "Dear Barnes Wallis," it read. "I was so distressed to hear your involuntary exclamation after the meeting yesterday. We

Catholics always pray to St Joseph when we are in special difficulty." He enclosed the wording of the prayer, and Wallis was not ashamed to say the prayer every morning for the next two months.

Even now Wallis was not given everything he needed. For a start, he had to have two hundred tons of steel billets to make the dies for the manufacture of the perfectly spherical bomb casings. This was refused him, and he had to content himself with designing the "Upkeep" version of the bombs as boilers, and padding them out to the spherical shape with wooden casing, held tightly in place by thick steel bands.

Conference followed conference. One spectre haunted him – the spectre of failure.

The A V Roe company's Roy Chadwick, the famous designer of the Avro Lancaster, came to discuss the bomber's necessary modification to carry the weapon; Group Captain Sidney Bufton arrived to work out the special bomber tactics to be used; armament experts came, to advise on the design of a pressure detonator (a hydrostatic pistol) robust enough to withstand the bomb's first 250 m.p.h. impact with the water, yet delicate enough to go off when the bomb had sunk precisely thirty feet. A V Roe promised to let Wallis have the first of the three experimental Lancasters by the first day of April 1943. Wallis moved in distraction between his secret country-house drawing office in the former Golf Club house at Burhill, the arsenal at Woolwich where the test bombs were being filled, and the experimental dropping grounds. Soon he was working ninety hours a week.

He himself designed and built the powerful calliper arms which were to grip each side of the rotating bomb as it was suspended in the Lancaster's bomb bay. He put to leading Government scientists like Professor Patrick Blackett complex questions like how much time would have to elapse before the waves on the Möhne lake's surface subsided after each bomb's detonation, should one bomb not be enough to breach the dam. On a test rig at Weybridge the four-foot bombs were spun at slowly increasing speeds then suddenly dropped into a specially-prepared pit of grease and sandbags to test the equipment's release action. All seemed to be going well.

On March 24, 1943 "Mutt" Summers drove down to Burhill, bringing a passenger with him in his little Fiat – a babyfaced Cornishman with smiling eyes and the uniform of an RAF Wing Commander.

Summers introduced him:

"This is Gibson – Guy Gibson."

"Gibson," wrote Wallis in his diary, "is doing the big job." Gibson had already survived doing 173 other "jobs" for Bomber Command, which made him a very rare bird indeed.

Of this first meeting with the bomb's inventor, Gibson himself later wrote:

"He looked around carefully before saying anything, then said abruptly but benignly over his thick spectacles:

"'I'm glad you've come; I don't suppose you know what for.'

"'No, I'm afraid not. SASO [Senior Air Staff Officer, Sir Robert Saundby] said you would tell me nearly everything, whatever that means.'

"He raised his eyebrows. 'Do you mean to say you don't know the target?' he asked.

"'Not the faintest idea.'

"'That makes it very awkward, very awkward. . . Only a very few people know, and no one can be told unless his name is on this list.'"

Wallis waved a list of names in front of Gibson. Gibson's name was not on it. The upshot was that the young

HEROES *Guy Gibson, the young commander of No. 617 Squadron, The Dambusters, and some of his men. Within two years, nearly all are dead*

NOT TO BE TAKEN INTO THE AIR.

Target No.
1 (j) 9

MÖHNE DAM — GÜNNE near SOEST (GERMANY)
G.S.G.S. 4416. Sheet Q 2.
RB 226214.
Lat. 51° 29' N.
Long. 08° 04' E.

Illustration No.
1 (j) 9/1

Pre-war photograph, date unknown

Re-issued January 1945

LOW OBLIQUE VIEW, LOOKING S.S.W.
Photographed before breaching of dam on 16/17 May 1943 when Power Station

THE DAM AND ITS NEMESIS. *The Möhne Dam, photographed before the war by British Intelligence. Barnes Wallis' secret bouncing bomb, suspended between two callipers beneath a Lancaster bomber, was given a powerful back spin before its release. One bomb is on display at Duxford war museum*

wing commander returned to his special squadron fully informed about the new bomb, and about the low-level tactics his bombers would have to employ, but with no idea as to what kind of target they would be attacking.

THE NEW BOMBER squadron, No. 617 Squadron, was formed at Scampton, late that March. Guy Gibson, recalled one of 617's pilots, was a magnificent squadron commander and his men followed him implicitly. "You either loved Gibson," said Dave Shannon, of the Royal Australian Air Force (RAAF), "or you were scared of him. He could be ruthless when the situation demanded it. . . He had an eye for the ladies, and off duty he was a great boozer." Shannon had been Gibson's co-pilot on many operations since June 1942 in No. 106 Squadron, and shared his hatred of "the Hun and all he stood for."

Gibson's pilots were all hand-picked men. He had called up Shannon and said, "I am starting up another squadron for a special raid. I can't tell you where or what it is, but if you'd like to join me again, I would only be too willing to have you back."

Another recruit was Tony Burcher, a rear gunner. Guy Gibson rang up Mickey Martin and asked if he would like to return to squadron duties – there was a special do on. "I understand, by the way, that Tony Burcher is over there with you. Bring him back as a gunner." When Burcher got to No. 617's mess he found John "Hoppy" Hopgood there. "Hoppy" had been his flight commander too, at No. 106. Burcher wrote in a letter: "I had assumed that I might be going back to fly with Mickey, but his two air gunners from his previous tour were there so obviously they flew with him and I attached myself with John's aircrew."

Gibson told them only that they were to practise low-level flying in three formations, that it was left to them what height they considered to be safe, and then, with a chuckle, that they were to consider 150 feet to be their *maximum* altitude. That was no picnic. A Lancaster's altimeter was known to be "pretty dicey" in those days.

He did not reveal to them for some weeks what they were going to be attacking – indeed, he himself did not even know yet. Late in April his men were told obliquely that that their target would be over water and they were to practice flying over lakes. His men assumed that the target would be Hitler's U-boat pens or battleships like *Scharnhorst*, *Gneisenau*, and even *Tirpitz*.

"At that time," recalled Shannon, "none of us, apart from Gibson, Leggo [Flight Lieutenant J F Leggo, RAAF], Hay [Flight Lieutenant R C Hay, RAAF], Trev [Flight Lieutenant R A D Trevor-Roper, RAFVR] and other section leaders were in the know. So we went and practised low flying over various lakes and reservoirs."

INTENSIVE TRAINING began, and soon complaints about low-level flying were cascading into the Bomber Group's headquarters. One angry local mayor said that he had seen motorists actually duck as formations of black-painted four-engined Lancasters thundered past only 150 feet up. Legend has it that Group HQ wrote back: "Our pilots have now been instructed to show due regard for other road-users. . . "

Late on April 6, 1943, the first special Lancaster was delivered to Farnborough; its mid-upper gun-turret had been removed, and unusual modifications had been made to the bomb bay. Now the first "Upkeep" bomb was clamped into position between the callipers, and the hydraulic motor coupled up to test the bomb's spin. That evening Wallis telephoned the RAF's new Controller of Research and Development, and told him that everything was "Okay."

All was ready for the Lancaster to begin the first drop-ping trials. "We'll try the first drop at about 270 m.p.h.," Wallis told the pilot, Sam Brown, "giving the bomb a back spin of about three hundred revs. Let it go when you are level, at 150 feet."

In confident mood, Barnes Wallis waited behind the little ruined church on the shore at Reculver on the north Kent coast, watching for the Lancaster. Wing Command-er Gibson drove up shortly and joined him, both of them shivering in the cold morning wind.

Soon they heard the familiar full-throated roar of Lan-caster engines in fine pitch. Brown, a civilian test pilot for A V Roe, the plane's manufacturer, was at the controls. Dead on time the big bomber appeared out of the low early-morning sun, followed by another Lancaster, slight-ly higher, carrying a cine-camera to record its progress. The first Lancaster had the bulky Dams Bomb suspended beneath it – the first that had ever been tested.

As the Lancasters neared the white marker-buoys a hundred yards off shore, Wallis began to shout, hope-lessly, into the roar of engines, "Sam, Sam, you're too high. You're too high!"

Gibson trained a pair of binoculars onto the bomb itself, chequered black and white and already spinning backwards at great speed. He had never seen anything like it. He wondered what on earth could be the target for such a remarkable device. He saw the bomb slowly detach itself from the Lancaster. "It seemed to hang in the air for a long time before it hit the water with a terrific splash," he wrote.

A plume of water sprang up out of the sea, missing the Lancaster by inches. But instead of bouncing, the bomb lurched briefly out of the boiling cauldron of spray, then sank without trace.

After lunch, a second bomb was dropped, with the bomber much lower than before; this time, the bomb suddenly disintegrated in a shower of wooden staves, steel bands and bolts, the heavy steel cylinder bursting out with such violence that one wooden segment smashed into the Lancaster's tail just above it, and nearly brought the aircraft down.

Sunk deep in thought, Wallis trudged with Gibson back through the shingle to where their cars were parked.

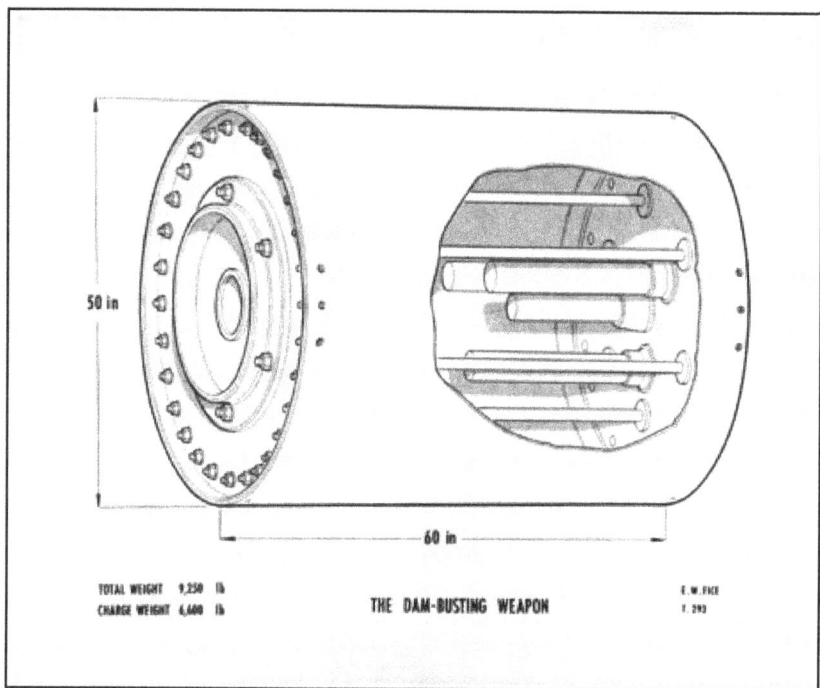

TOTAL WEIGHT   9,250   lb
CHARGE WEIGHT 6,600   lb

THE DAM-BUSTING WEAPON

E. W. PACE
T. 293

Chapter Two: In which Mr Barnes Wallis gets the special bomb to work, and the raid begins

British inventor-extraordinary Barnes Wallis shivered as the sea slowly rose to his neck. I'm getting beyond this sort of thing, he thought.

He and a handful of middle-aged men dressed only in underpants were slowly edging their way out from the beach. Had anybody else been strolling down that deserted Reculver shore in Kent that chilly April evening, it would have been a strange sight that met his eyes.

But there were no onlookers. It was wartime. This was April 17, 1943, and all access roads to this secluded spot had been cordoned off by sentries all day.

Wallis was one of the foremost aeronautical engineers in Britain. The other bathers were leading scientists and civil servants.

"It's no use," sighed Wallis after a while. "We've been looking for hours. The fragments must all be buried far too deep. Let's go back to the Miramar for dinner – I'm getting cold."

They were looking for the remains of a ball that they had lost – a four-ton spherical bomb. A low-flying Lancaster bomber had dropped it in the sea, but instead of bouncing along on the surface of the sea, it had shattered and sunk before their eyes.

The bouncing bomb was Wallis's invention – an invention with which he hoped to destroy the Germans' heavily-guarded power and water supply dams, vital to the Ruhr where most of Germany's heavy industry was concentrated. "An Engineer's Way to Win the War" was how he had described it.

"I just don't understand it," he said to mathematician Professor Taylor, as he recovered his thick, horn-rimmed spectacles from his pile of clothes and replaced them on his nose. "We gave the bomb the right amount of back spin. We dropped it from the right height, and at the right speed. And yet – crunch – it falls to pieces."

He shivered in the cold spring air, as he dried himself on the only thing available, a large pocket handkerchief. He was in no doubt as to the bleak future. The whole operation – crews, aircraft and bombs – had to be perfect by May 10, 1943, which was less than four weeks from now. Only then would the moon be full – and the enemy reservoirs.

For three years he had campaigned for the recognition of his project, and now at last people had listened to him. He had blown-up scale models of dams and shown that his shockwave theory of destroying them held, but only so long as the bombs could be exploded in contact with the dam wall. He had developed small-scale bombs that would bounce over the defences, and cling to the dam wall as they sunk. Colossal sums of money were being invested in the operation now – not just the £400 his tiny model-dam experiments at the Road Research Laboratory had cost.

Against military and civil-service opposition, Mr Churchill had intervened and ordered the establishment of a special Lancaster bomber squadron, and that unit, No. 617 Squadron, was even now training for the one task of destroying the five major Ruhr dams. Twenty-one Lancaster bombers had been taken off the production line at Avro's and drastically modified to carry the special spherical bomb that he, Wallis, had promised would do the trick.

So now there was only one snag: the full-scale bomb was a failure. The first time they had dropped it, a monster steel cylinder padded out to the shape of a sphere with wooden packing, it had burst as soon as it struck the sea. That was no good at all.

ON THE DAY AFTER their fruitless bathing party, Wallis and the other experts watched three more full-scale bombs dropped in the English Channel off Reculver by the same Lancaster. Two had been given a special varnish coating, and the third was finished in plain wood. On the first run, the sphere stayed intact but sank immediately, without bouncing. The second bomb shattered into fragments, just like the one they had dropped some days before.

Wallis groaned, and steeled himself for the failure of the third.

As the Lancaster roared past this time, something unexpected happened. The bomb hit the sea, and the wooden casing completely disintegrated just as before. But the bare steel cylinder was left, still madly spinning, and this burst out of the tower of spray and hopped quite clearly several times across the sea, covering finally a distance of seven hundred yards.

"The sphere broke up," exclaimed Walls, speaking more to himself than to the others. "But the *cylinder* ran just as it should have done! It ran!"

He gave orders for full-size bombs to be manufactured keeping the steel cylinder shape, but bare of any kind of wooden casing. Early on April 22, the Lancaster test-dropped one of them off the same deserted beach from a height of 185 feet. This test too was a failure, but Wallis was sure he knew a way of licking the problem. His staff saw him reach for his slide-rule and a pad of paper.

Two days later, he met with Wing Commander Guy Gibson, 617 Squadron's commander, and put it to him.

"I know this is asking an awful lot," Wallis said hesitantly. "You must tell me at once if it can't be done. Can you bring your planes down to a level sixty feet, instead of 150, and make exactly 232 miles an hour, before you release your bomb?"

Gibson swallowed hard. He thought, If 150 feet is low, then sixty feet is *very* low. At that height you've only got to hiccup to land in the drink.

But he loyally replied, "We'll have a crack tonight."

When the morning chosen for the final crucial trials dawned, it was pouring with rain and there was a freezing wind. Wallis and the Air Ministry experts again crowded the foreshore at Reculver beach.

Just sixty feet up, the black Lancaster bomber roared past them. As the bare steel cylinder dropped from its bomb bay, spinning backwards, and slowly fell towards the sea, Wallis silently prayed.

It struck the sea with a crash – and emerged from the plume of spray making a gigantic bounce. The bomb bounced, bounced, and bounced again – each time striding hundreds of yards forward and throwing up huge spouts of water as though an invisible giant was stamping across the sea. Then it settled, and sank from sight.

Wallis had done it!

In his mind's eye, at the moment that his "bouncing bomb" disappeared from view, Barnes Wallis could see a huge masonry wall looming across the horizon, towering up out of the waves – a wall suddenly rent by blast and collapsing under the weight of millions of tons of water: the Möhne Dam.

Then the others were crowding round him, clapping him on the back and congratulating him. Wallis allowed himself a cautious smile, as he returned to his car.

ONE TRIAL ALONE was not enough, of course. Other tests followed, to get the speed of the aircraft and the amount of back spin imparted to the bomb just right.

A means had to be found for aircraft to fly at precisely sixty feet over smooth water by night – an apparently suicidal task. Then someone remembered that a similar problem had been solved by an inventor in the First World War, who had proposed mounting two Aldis lamps, spotlights, underneath a plane at its nose and belly, angled so that their beams would only intersect at a certain height. In a surprisingly short space of time the actual apparatus was found gathering dust in a store at Farnborough, and the contraption was adapted for Guy Gibson's squadron.

After testing this strange device over empty airfields, the crews went out over the Wash, getting down as low as they could, and soon they were hitting targets only six feet across with practice bombs, an accuracy almost unheard-of in those days.

One day early in May, a Lancaster dropped the first special bomb to be fully charged with its explosive: a huge pillar of water shot up, towering hundreds of feet into the sky. Barnes Wallis's work on the weapon was complete; everything was now up to Gibson and his crews.

A number of his men flew down to Kent to drop a dummy version of the bomb over the sea off Reculver. They had to get the feel of how their Lancasters would react, particularly to the gyroscopic forces unleashed by nine thousand pounds of revolving steel before the bomb was released. The vibration was intense.

"You had to try and hold the plane steady," said Shannon. "Our only target was a couple of posts on the beach." The posts marked the separation of the towers on the Möhne dam. "We had to fly towards them . . . get down to the height and line up with them, with a handheld 'V' bombsight, which would determine the distance we were away, before we dropped the weapon. When released [it] behaved like a flat stone that skimmed across the water from your childhood" – like Ducks & Drakes, in fact, but deadlier.

Seventy-two hours ahead of the operation the special weapons were delivered to No. 617 Squadron's crews. Until the modified Lancaster aircraft were actually flown in, the men had trained on the conventional Lancasters. The bomb itself looked to them like the heavy front roller of a steamroller. To rear-gunner Tony Burcher it looked more like a giant jam tin.

*

At three o'clock on the afternoon of Saturday May 15, 1943 Wallis climbed into a white Wellington aircraft with his Chief Test Pilot "Mutt" Summers and Major Kilner, Vickers' managing director. There was a big Red Cross on the aircraft's sides – it was the only plane available.

In brooding silence, the little party flew from Vickers' aerodrome at Weybridge up to the operational bomber station at Scampton. Eighteen of No. 617 squadron's nineteen specially modified black Lancaster bombers were already waiting at their dispersal areas.

Guy Gibson met Wallis as he climbed down the Wellington's ladder. "The AOC's just told me we're doing the job tomorrow night, if the weather holds," he said.

Wallis nodded absently, unable to believe that after three years of an increasingly frustrating battle against bureaucracy, the day had come when 133 hand-picked RAF officers and men were to stake their lives on the accuracy of his calculations. How could he express his feelings to these men? He was nearly sixty – they were almost without exception under twenty-three; young, carefree, and eager.

Young though they were, their faces wore the battle-hardened expressions of veterans. All had completed two tours of bomber operations, so there were no greenhorns among them: all had been decorated, and all were experts in their deadly crafts. They were the elite.

The weather forecast was favourable. There would be moonlight over the targets. "Security was very tight," recalled one pilot. "No telephoning out, all mail was censored or held over." For weeks Guy Gibson had threatened to broadcast over the station's Tannoy system any letter that contained any classified information. "There were some pretty juicy letters being written in those days to girl friends," said the pilot. Gibson threatened to do the same with telephone messages – that he'd read the whole conversation out. One of the officers was dismissed for breaching security – he was found to have telephoned his girl friend on the day before the operation. Gibson could be both brutal and coldly efficient. He called a full parade, and dismissed the man in front of the squadron. Their mission was already dangerous enough. Secrecy was essential. Nothing else mattered.

There would be nineteen crews, flying in three formations. Now for the first time they learned of their real targets for the raid, the dams. There was general relief that it was not the Nazi battleships. Several of these airmen had seen action against them as they escaped up the English Channel in February 1942: "I actually saw the Halifaxes bombing them," said Tony Burcher, who was an air gunner in the elderly Hampden bombers at the time. "They had a umbrella of Messerschmitt 109's over them and the Halifaxes were being chopped to pieces. I had never seen so much flak in all my life." Nobody had relished the idea of going in to attack these battleships at a height of sixty feet. The Ruhr dams sounded quite harmless. Surely they would not be nearly so well defended?

The wraps were taken off contour scale models of the Möhne Dam, the Eder Dam, and the Sorpe Dam and the airmen were instructed to study them. Officers briefed

them on the targets' strategic significance and the enemy's night-fighter and flak defences along the flight
routes.

At six o'clock, Barnes Wallis faced the nineteen cap-
tains of aircraft for the first time: chalk in hand, standing on a platform in the almost empty Briefing Hall, the
inventor repeated the now-familiar explanation of the
crucial importance of the Ruhr Dams to Hitler's war industry. Then he gave them the scientific theory.

"Your airspeed at the time of release must be 220 mph
and your altitude exactly 60 feet. The distance at right
angles over the water, back from the dam wall, is exactly
410 yards. The bomb will bounce three times, arrive at
the dam, roll down the face of the dam to a depth of
thirty feet and explode."

As he spoke, Wallis recalled how many times he had
appealed for this attack before. What if there were some
unconsidered factor even now, which would prove his
theories wrong? The effect of gravity in such an enormous structure as the Möhne Dam, for example. It did
not bear thinking of.

Wallis finished his lecture. He slowly surveyed the cu-
rious faces through his spectacles, and said: "You see, you

gentlemen are really carrying out the third of three great experiments: we have tried this out on model dams, and we have tried it out on a dam one-fifth the size of the Möhne. I can't guarantee that it will come off. But I hope it will. . . "

Heavy eight-wheeled trucks were rolling across the airfield as he left the Briefing Hall. Each was laden with the big cylindrical bombs, covered with tarpaulins, and each was still warm from the four tons of special high-explosive cast inside it at Woolwich Arsenal.

In Guy Gibson's crowded office, the final plans were hatched. Code-words had to be arranged, last-minute alterations to bomber routes worked out. He and Wallis stayed there until after midnight. This time tomorrow Gibson would already be over the Möhne Dam, and Wallis would know whether his calculations had been correct.

*

It was far into Sunday morning before Barnes Wallis woke up. It was a balmy, sunny day such as seldom comes in May. He breakfasted late, and spent the afternoon fussing round the special Lancasters. Each crew wanted him to see if their bomb was spinning properly. At mid-day, the last of the special Lancasters arrived, brand-new from Avro's. Nineteen aircraft and crews were now ready.

At three o'clock, the clattering fingers of the teleprinters at Scampton slammed into the paper roll, repeating a signal from No. 5 Bomber Group Headquarters:

CODE NAME FOR FIVE GROUP OPERATION ORDER B.976 IS "CHASTISE"

Ten minutes later the die was finally cast for that night:

EXECUTIVE, OPERATION "CHASTISE," 16 MAY 1943, ZERO HOUR 11.48.

Three hours later, behind locked doors, Wallis again briefed the bomber crews. They looked tired and strained, and small wonder: in two months of intensive training for "Chastise" they had completed nearly two thousand hours of nerve-racking low-level cross-country flight, most of it in darkness.

As they trooped out of the Briefing Hall, Wallis turned to Gibson, his voice strained. "I hope that you all come back," he said.

"It won't be your fault if we don't," came the reply.

GIBSON'S SECOND IN COMMAND, twenty-three year old Flight Lieutenant John Hopgood, captain of Lancaster AJ–M, called out:

"Hey, Gibby. If you don't come back, can I have your egg tomorrow?"

It was the oldest of the RAF's aircrew gags. It masked Hopgood's own special anxiety. Before his crew climbed into their Lancaster, he explained to them, "The first aircraft to attack the dam will probably catch the flak gunners with their pants down. But the second won't be so lucky – and that's us."

He tugged at Dave Shannon's sleeve and held him back for a final cigarette together behind a hangar.

Shannon, commander of AJ–L, liked Hopgood. He was a sensitive, compassionate, and brave Englishman who had once wept openly after accidentally killing a pigeon while doing target practice with some bottles and his Webley service revolver. The bird had been so innocent and harmless. Before No. 617 Squadron, he and Shannon had come from the same bomber squadron, No. 106, where he had been Shannon's flight commander.

For a few minutes Hopgood puffed his cigarette silently, then he blurted out in his soft voice: "I think this is going to be a tough one, David. I don't think I'm coming back."

It shook his friend to hear it said in such a matter-of-fact way.

"Come off it, Hoppy!" he said. "You'll beat these bastards! You've beaten them for so long, you're not going to get whipped tonight.'

Hopgood stubbed the cigarette out, and they walked over to their planes.

Medics were issuing cod-liver oil and tablets, "tables to help you stay awake," they said (they were caffeine and the stimulant Benzedrine).

Heavy with flying gear and equipment, the rest of the men walked down to the flight line. Tony Burcher also had a premonition, and briefly turned back to fetch one of the bottles of Horlicks tablets his mother routinely sent from Australia, believing that Britain was starving. He now had an unused store of this malted milk in a drawer in his quarters. He tucked the bottle into an inside pocket, and never regretted it.

At nine-thirty p.m. Wallis stood on the airfield and watched as the heavy bombers, pregnant with his top-secret bombs, lumbered down the runway like a herd of elephants, trunk to tail, and waited for their signals to blink from the control tower. None but the crews knew that this was the real thing. There was not even the usual farewell party of WAAFs and ground crew to wave them off.

Soon the last aircraft had lifted into the moonlight air. "We stood silently until the final sounds of their engines died away," described one WAAF aircraftwoman. "Then we all drifted away to our duties. "There was no sleep for anyone that night, our hearts and minds were in those planes. We WAAFs just sat waiting, we had laid out the tables and a hot meal would be ready on their return."

As the night wore on, they twice heard the roar of Merlin engines and rushed outside. Two of the Lancs were returning early. The girls wandered back in once more to wait. The WAAF sergeant made them coffee and calmed them down: "It will not be long now before our boys start to come back" she said. The Lincolnshire mist of late spring rolled across the almost-empty airfield.

BARNES WALLIS WANDERED into the Officers Mess, but his appetite for dinner was almost gone. He wondered how many of these young men would return. By the time he had finished his meal, seven had already died – obliterated in a sheet of flame as Lancaster K for Kite, flown by Sergeant G W Byers, struck the Waddenzee lake in Holland, brought down by a Nazi flak battery based on one of the offshore Dutch islands. He had been flying at three hundred feet instead of the sixty feet ordered, and perhaps that proved his undoing.

At two minutes past eleven, the first two waves of No. 617 squadron's bombers swept in across the enemy coast at points widely separated, so as to divide the Luftwaffe fighter forces.

As Guy Gibson's own little group, the three Lancasters in the vanguard – Gibson, Hopgood, and Micky Martin – reached the lakes near Haltern, they ran into an unexpected nest of searchlights and flak guns. Within seconds, all three aircraft were caught in a dazzling cone of searchlight beams.

Gibson threw his aircraft to one side and got out unscathed. Tony Burcher, rear gunner in Flight Lieutenant Hopgood's M for Mother, cheerfully rattled his machine guns at the searchlights.

This may have provoked retaliation – Burcher always fretted about that afterwards – as the bomber suddenly shuddered as light flak shells tore into the port wing.

"Anyway," reflected Burcher guiltily afterwards, "regardless of what may or may not have happened had I fired or not, John Hopgood was hit." The cannon shells exploded in the cockpit, and over the intercom the rest of the crew heard Hoppy's flight engineer Sergeant Charlie Brennan gasp, "Bloody Hell. . . !"

Their front gunner George Gregory was evidently already dead. Hoppy had been hit in the face, and blood was pumping out of the open wound. Hoppy's grim prediction was coming true. Clutching the control column, he shouted to Charlie, "Don't worry. Hold your handkerchief against it."

Minutes passed. Forbidden by intercom etiquette to inquire what was happening, and cramped in the rear gun turret, Burcher listened in anguish to the grunts of pain and metallic voices ringing in his earphones.

"Right. Well, what do you think?"

That was Hopgood again. "Should we go on? I intend to, because we have only got a few minutes left. We've come this far."

More minutes passed without answer, then: "There's no good taking this thing back with us," and Burcher could imagine Hoppy jerking a bloody thumb down at the special bomb hanging motionless beneath them. "The aircraft is completely manageable. I can handle it okay. Any objections?"

Charlie Brennan, normally a level-headed chap, responded, "Well, what about your face? Its bleeding like –"

Hoppy cut off the rest of the words and ordered: "Just hold a handkerchief over it."

Burcher could imagine Charlie standing next to Hopgood, holding the bandage to staunch the bleeding and keep the blood out of his eyes. It was obviously a head injury and a severe one at that.

Anyone else would probably have turned around at that point, said Burcher later, and headed for home – but not Hopgood. That was the kind of guy he was. It was what heroes were made of.

Hoppy switched on the VHF radio, and called up Gibson: "We've been hit, Sir. But we're carrying on. see you on target."

He checked on his crew one by one: there was no reply from the front gunner.

So Gregory must have bought it, thought Burcher.

———————

THE AIRCRAFT WERE now flying so low that accidents were bound to happen. One Lancaster dropped so low over the Zuyder Zee that the bomb suspended beneath its bomb bay was torn off by a wave. The plane actually swallowed a huge gulp of salt water but the pilot, Flying Officer Geoff Rice, managed to stay aloft and brought it back to Scampton with his rear-gunner half-drowned by the flood. That was one plane the WAAFs had heard returning. Still the remaining aircraft swept on across the moonlit plains.

The noise on the ground must have been deafening. Through a reddening cloud of pain Flight Lieutenant Hopgood saw that he was heading straight for a line of pylons. He was only sixty feet up. He took a split-second decision. He eased his column forwards, and swooped beneath the cables; as the tail of the bomber went up, rear gunner Pilot Officer Tony Burcher thought they had had it. He saw the shadows of the cables whip across the top of his turret, and then the danger was past.

The leader of the second wave, Flight Lieutenant Bill Astell, lost his way soon after midnight: it was only for a moment, but it was long enough to kill him and his crew. After crossing a canal he had to turn south briefly to try to find a landmark, and he was shot down almost at once by machine-gunners on Gilze-Rijen airfield. Out of control, his Lancaster Mark III, B for Baker, crashed into a block of barracks on the airfield's edge and blew up in a slow red glare that momentarily swelled to light up the whole sky. The other Lancaster crews saw the clouds of smoke, but these faded into the distance until they were out of sight of the rest of the formation.

In G for George, Wing Commander Guy Gibson risked a glance at his watch. Quarter past midnight. "Well, boys, we'd better start the ball rolling!"

He meant it literally. The flight engineer flicked a switch on the two-stroke motor driving the mechanism, and with gathering momentum the special bomb suspended between powerful calliper jaws in the bomb bay began to revolve. A few minutes later, the flight engineer reported: "Five hundred revs, Sir."

Gibson switched on his transmitter: "All aircraft switch over to radiotelephone control."

Ahead of him he could see the rolling hills of the Ruhr coming towards them. He lifted the Lancaster up and cleared the first with feet to spare. There was a shout from his bomb-aimer.

"We're there!"

There ahead of them was the Möhne lake, and at its far end, silhouetted against the moonlight, was the Dam, 2,100 feet long. The lake was so full that its parapet barely showed above the water's mirrorlike surface.

"Good God – can we break that?" gasped Gibson.

With its low freeboard and two stone towers the Möhne Dam looked like an enormous and impregnable battleship, and the battleship was angry: it was firing a broadside at them from twelve or fifteen guns, and there were more guns on the lake's north shore. The glowing onion-strings of deadly tracer fire streamed across the lake, aimlessly as yet because the aircraft were hard to see and echoes were reverberating from every hill.

Gibson called up each of his force's Lancasters in turn. All but Bill Astell reported in.

Astell had been dead twenty-five minutes by now.

"Hullo all aircraft. I'm going in to attack. Stand by to come in to attack in your order when I tell you. . . "

It was precisely twenty-eight minutes past midnight. Gibson brought his Lancaster round, and dived over the woods fringing the lake. His bomb-aimer "Spam" Spafford shouted, "You're going to hit those trees."

"That's all right, Spam – I'm just getting my height."

His navigator Terry Taerum switched on the two spotlights, nose and underbelly. This was when things could get really dangerous. He watched the two short lines projected onto the lake just in front of the plane. They were still some way apart.

"Down . . . down . . . down. . . " he directed.

Gibson shifted in his seat nervously, as water came up toward the thundering plane. "That's it!" came Terry's voice. "Steady now."

They were just sixty feet up. "Spam" clicked the bomb's fusing switches into the "On" position.

A mile ahead of them, one of the German gunners shouted, "They've switched on their landing lights! They must be mad!"

A hail of fire swept out from the crest of the dam, converging on the advancing aircraft. Crouched behind his controls, Gibson thought, In another twenty seconds we shall all be dead.

Spafford hit the bomb release and yelled, "Bomb gone!"

The black cylinder slipped out of its clamps. Engines thundering, the bomber lurched upwards as its load fell away. The bomb struck the lake, bounced once . . .

twice . . . three times, covering a hundred yards with each enormous bound. The weapon slammed into the dam's parapet, right between the valve towers – a magnificent shot. The bomb ricocheted backwards, and sank into the lake.

The seconds began to tick away.

Gibson's wireless operator had fired a red Verey cartridge as they crossed the dam. As the flare soared up into the sky, there was a colossal explosion and a column of water and spray mushroomed up into the sky, towering above the dam. It was the most fantastic spectacle they had ever seen – this silver moonlit column of water, lit a lurid red on one side by the red signal flare.

But the dam was still holding.

Gibson ordered his radio operator to signal England using the prearranged code, that they had released the special bomb; that it had exploded only five yards from the dam; and that the dam had not been broken.

*

Shortly before midnight, a large black saloon car swept up to the guardroom at No. 5 Group's headquarters at

Grantham. The driver flashed special recognition lamps at the sentries. The sentries stood back and allowed the car to pass at once.

This was Air Chief Marshal Sir Arthur Harris, the fearsome Commander in Chief of Bomber Command – best known as "Butcher" Harris.

He strode into the Headquarters Operations Room. Barnes Wallis was already there. He had been driven over from the Scampton airfield an hour before.

"Any news yet?" barked Harris. He was a gruff Rhodesian.

"Apart from an early flak warning from Gibson there's nothing at all," answered Air Vice-Marshal Cochrane, the Group commander. "But they should be attacking at any moment."

One of the room's long walls was dominated by a chalkboard listing the bombers taking part, like horses in a race. On a dais running along the opposite wall sat the operations officers, in telephone contact with the wireless room.

Barnes Wallis had long ceased pacing up and down, and was now sitting in a dejected heap on the little staircase leading up to the dais.

John Fraser

Hoppy Hopgood

Joe McCarthy

Terry Taerum, RCAF

The Eder dam was well known to British Intelligence, from its collection of holiday postcards – now marked up with target identifiers by RAF Bomber Command

Below. *The theory behind the Bouncing Bomb*

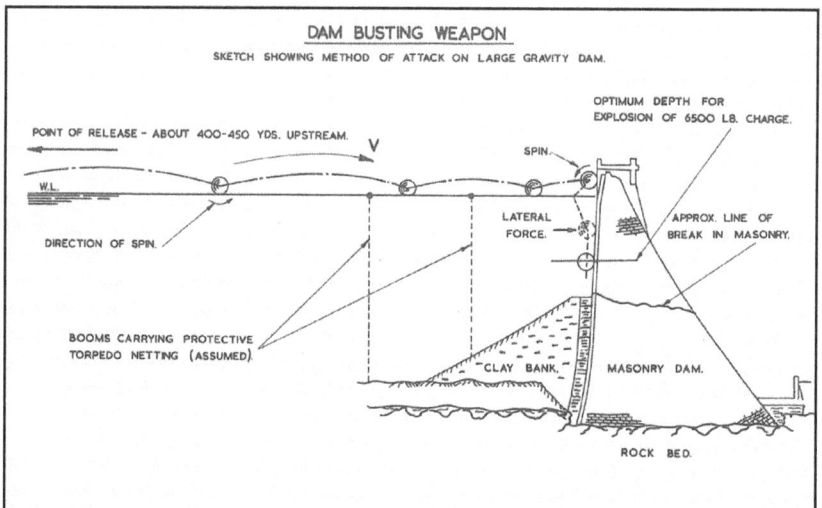

On May 17, 1943, a plane of No. 542 Squadron brought back photographs of the Möhne Dam showing the result of the night's attack

A grim sight greeted locals on the morning of May 17, 1943 – millions of tons of water cascading from the breached Möhne Dam.

Harris joined the Group commander at the other end of the room, underneath the map of Europe.

Suddenly there was a shout.

"There's a signal just coming through, Sir." The Chief Signals Officer had a telephone to his ear. "It's from Wing Commander Gibson: GONER – bomb exploded five yards from dam, no apparent breach."

He waited. Then he added: "That's all."

So Gibson's bomb had been correctly placed, but the dam was still standing. An icy chill gripped Wallis: all those lives, he thought.

He buried his head in his clammy hands; out of the corner of his eye he could see the two air marshals at the far end of the room, and there was a perceptible look of vexation invading "Butcher" Harris's features.

ALONE IN THE 6,000-kilowatt powerhouse below the Möhne Dam, there was a look of fear on 52-year-old foreman Clement Köhler's face. Now there was no doubt at all. The British were attacking his dam.

A look-out on the Bismarck Tower had raised the alarm at twenty minutes past midnight, just as the first Lancaster had begun circling the lake. At first the small but wiry foreman had not been afraid – air-raid warnings were not uncommon in the Ruhr by 1943.

But suddenly something clicked in his mind: tonight there was a full moon, and the RAF did not normally venture over the Ruhr on moonlight nights. And tonight the lake's level was higher than it had ever been before.

Soon his fears were confirmed. The British bombers were not droning past high overhead – they were swarming like stray bees around the distant end of his lake, and one was coming nearer.

Köhler's hand reached for the telephone. With trembling fingers he dialled the number of the United Electricity Company of Westphalia offices in Nierderense and Neheim – the little towns just down the valley. The noise of aircraft engines was very loud now.

Hoarse with fear, he shouted: "This time they are attacking the dam!"

The voice at the other end was sleepy at first, and downright disbelieving. Köhler slammed the phone down, and ran for the door.

As he tore the door open, he caught the sound of the guns on both towers firing wildly and then Guy Gibson's Lancaster thundered over him, barely a hundred feet up, the whole valley vibrating to the thunder of its four Rolls-Royce Merlin engines. A huge explosion tore at Köhler's lungs, and water cascaded over the top of the dam.

Drenched to the skin, Köhler began to run – he ran as he had never run before until he had reached the side of the valley hundreds of yards away; and then flopped down underneath a larch-tree half-way up the slopes. He turned round, and gazed as though hypnotised at the enormous dam wall's moonlit face. It was still not cracked.

GIBSON WAS RADIOING the second of his aircraft to go into the attack.

"Hello, M for Mother. Make your attack now. Good luck!"

Hoppy Hopgood, his face numb from loss of blood, grunted: "Okay, attacking."

Over his aircraft intercom he ordered: "Stand by, rear gunner. They're putting up a terrific barrage ahead."

The German gunners on the dam knew just what to do now. They were throwing up a curtain of deadly fire between the two towers through which the attackers would have to pass. Facing aft, Pilot Officer Tony Burcher, M for

Mother's rear gunner, couldn't see much yet, just the onion-strings of tracer fire flashing past him on both sides. His biggest worry was not of the enemy defences, but his fear that his mates might find out just how scared he was.

In fact, there was too much going on all around now to be really scared. Their plane had sprung a glycol leak. It had lost power after the earlier shell-hit but somehow Hoppy had kept the defective port engine going; he had not feathered it, but he had reduced the revs to avoid worse.

Burcher moistened his lips and watched the lake surface coming up towards his turret. Streams of tracer and cannon-shell flashed past as the Lancaster raced in towards the dam.

He swung his turret round to one side, ready to open fire on the dam's gunners as soon as they came into his field of fire. George, the front gunner is not firing, Burcher now realised. He must be dead already.

Over the intercom could hear the navigator telling the pilot to take her down lower – and then lower still.

Suddenly there was a whummmph, and sparks and flames streamed past Burcher's turret. A fuel tank had been hit.

"Christ! The engine's on fire!" shouted the engineer.

"Feather Number Two," ordered Hopgood. He was going by the book. "Press the extinguisher."

The Canadian Pilot Officer John W Fraser, released the special bomb about a fifth of a second too late. Perhaps he was startled. Bounding across the lake it shot over the parapet of the dam and blew up in a vivid yellow flash.

"Right. Prepare to abandon aircraft," and shortly after that: "Right, everybody get out". That was Hoppy's voice again. There was no hint of fear, no trace of emotion; he sounded calm and at ease, as though nothing was wrong. He was a professional to the end.

Burcher heard the order and desperately tried to swing his turret round to the fore-and-aft position, but the hydraulics were powered by a pick-up on the port-inner engine and that engine was now dead, a mass of flames. The turret motor wouldn't budge. He felt a terrific shuddering going throughout the doomed aircraft. She was in her death throes.

"I'm trapped." His parachute pack was hanging inside the fuselage, and he could not get at it until the turret was fore-and-aft. Parachute! What use was a parachute at sixty feet?

Like a man possessed he began to crank the Dead Man's Handle, inching the turret round by hand. Never had he operated that handle so fast in his life before, but now his life depended on it.

Up front in the cockpit, mopping the blood away from his eyes, the Lancaster's commander clung grimly to the control column with his free hand. Both of the magnificent Rolls-Royce Merlin engines on the port wing were now dead. The plane was losing power and even with their bomb-load gone he could not gain real altitude. He would never get out alive himself.

As for Charlie Brennan, calm until the very end, he kept pressing the bandage against his friend's head injury. There was one last service which these two men could perform for their crew: hauling on the control column, Hoppy banked the Lancaster steeply round to the right on their two good engines, away from the valley which was doomed to be drowned.

GIBSON'S OTHER CREWS had seen the red Verey cartridge fired by Hopgood's radio operator Sergeant John W Minchin as the bomb went. Now they were transfixed by the horrifying sight of the Lancaster flown by Flight

Lieutenant Hopgood, the gentle English boy they had all come to like so well, plunging on into the night, streaming a growing plume of flame.

The plane was climbing steeply to the starboard, using her dying momentum. Somehow Hoppy hauled her up to about three hundred feet. Burcher had scrambled inside the main fuselage, and was struggling to strap on his parachute.

The rear hatch flew open. He saw that Sergeant Minchin had opened it. His right leg shot away, the radio operator had dragged himself along the fuselage. He had even got over the main spar somehow.

Burcher could have jumped now, but he saw that Minchin was dragging his own parachute by one hand. He grabbed the chute and fastened it properly onto the white-faced, dying man. He tore open the jump door and held on to the chute's D-ring as he hurled his comrade out into the roaring slipstream. He did not see any chute opening. He had nightmares for years afterwards about whether he had done the right thing.

Still inside the plane, Burcher pulled his own ripcord and bundled as much of the silk parachute under his arm as he could. Then, in one final mechanical act – the act of an officer exceptionally well drilled – he plugged into the intercom socket by the rear hatch and gasped, "Rear gunner, abandoning ship now!"

He heard Hoppy scream, "For Christ's sake, get ***** out of here!"

They were the last words he spoke. M for Mother erupted in a sheet of flame as the fires reached back to the high-octane fuel in the main wing fuel tanks. Burcher was blasted up into the air, his back broken by the bomber's tail-fin. Less than three hundred feet below, the ground rushed up to meet him, and a painful darkness enveloped his consciousness.

CHAPTER THREE: In which the Ruhr Dams
are breached

Pilot officer Anthony Burcher, Royal Australian Air Force and twenty-one years old, lay in a crumpled heap in the middle of what felt like a newly ploughed field. He opened his eyes, and saw the moon and stars.

"Good God," he thought. "I'm still alive!" Echoing around the valley he could hear the familiar growl of Lancaster bomber engines. He wondered what had happened to his own aircraft, M for Mother; not so many minutes ago, he had been crouching in its rear gun-turret, watching the sheet of water flash past sixty feet beneath him and the streams of tracer shells streak by on either side.

He felt hungry. Instinctively, he thrust his hand inside his blue polo-neck sweater and felt for the bottle of Horlicks tablets. His mother, back in Goulburn, Australia, had heard that everybody in England was starving, and every month she sent her boy Tony a supply of the tablets to keep him going until he could return to the outback. His locker back at Scampton was full of them. Hell, he was glad of the impulse that had made him pick up a box of them on his way over to the briefing hall.

The briefing hall . . . In a rush it all came back to him. His Lancaster had been one of nineteen sent out by No. 617 Squadron with the task of destroying five vital barrage dams that supplied the Ruhr arms factories with all their water. M for Mother had been the second to attack the first target, the biggest dam of them all – the Möhne dam. But they had been hit by flak, right over the dam, and blown up only about three hundred feet up. How had he survived?

He remembered helping Johnny Minchin to jump – actually he had thrown him out – and then squatting on the step by the Lanc's open door. This was no height to

ILL

parachute from. He had pulled the D-ring before jumping, which was a stupid thing to do at any other time than this. Then the plane had blown up – he had felt a great rush of air and then a hell of whack across his back. Normally he would have gone straight out beneath the bomber's tail fin but he must have been going up rather down, and the top of the tail fin had smashed into him.

That broke his back, but it also saved him that night, because the jolt dragged his parachute right out after him, and part-filled the canopy. The doomed Lancaster was in a banking turn to starboard. He felt the familiar jerk as the chute opened and hit the ground at the same instant.

Now Tony Burcher lay in the middle of a freshly ploughed field, which also cushioned his fall. If he felt lucky, it was not for long.

With a dull sense of inevitable disaster, he realised that somewhere up the valley from where he lay there was the dam, which even now his comrades-in-arms were trying to breach. In a few minutes he was going to get very wet indeed, unless he could run. But his back felt as if it were broken, and he had smashed one knee cap too.

Man's instinct, if he has to die, is to die unseen. With

"DINGHY" *Young's plane, shot down near Castricum as he flew home.*

THE ONE THAT GOT AWAY: *E for Easy's unexploded 9,500 pound "Upkeep" bomb was found near Haldern. The Germans built copies, but they didn't work: they were spinning the wrong way.*

PROPAGANDA *The British press was jubilant at the news. The exploit gave a great boost to British public morale.*

In fact the damage to the dams and bridges was repaired far faster than Barnes Wallis and British Intelligence had estimated. Adolf Hitler's munitions minister Albert Speer (below, dining with the author in 1979) oversaw an unprecedented effort to rebuild the dams.

AFTER US THE DELUGE *The Eder dam after the attack – and before.*
Millions of tons of water engulfed the streets of little towns in the
valley. Over a thousand people died.

enormous difficulty Burcher dragged his broken body across the field and hid in a culvert going under a road at its edge, and here he lapsed back into unconsciousness.

Just a mile away from him the 23,000 souls in the valley town of Neheim-Hüsten waited in their basements and air-raid shelters – waited for sirens to sound the All Clear, unaware that tonight the RAF was attacking the dams above them.

THE BOMB DROPPED by Hopgood's Lancaster Mark III, M for Mother, just before she blew up had bounded right over the dam's parapet and crashed onto the roof of the powerhouse below. Smoke from the burning building mingled with the spray thrown up by the earlier detonations on the lake side of the dam, and obscured the whole target area. Some minutes ticked past before Wing Commander Guy Gibson felt it proper to continue the attack.

A few minutes after half-past midnight, he ordered Flight Lieutenant Micky Martin to attack in P for Popsy, as Martin unofficially dubbed his aircraft. The night air was now heavy with spray, and it clung to the aircraft windshields; at first Martin's bomb-aimer Flight Lieutenant R C Hay could not see the target properly at all –

just the distant blurred glow of M for Mother's wreckage burning in the hills about two miles beyond the dam.

Even as the range closed to just over a mile, he could see only one of the dam's two distinctive valve-towers through the dense cloud of dust and smoke. He needed both to get the range right.

Wing Commander Gibson realised that Martin's best hope of success was for the enemy gunners' attention to be distracted. He switched on all his own aircraft's lights and flew alongside the attacking Lancaster, blazing away at the defences with the dazzling 100-per-cent night-tracer in his guns.

At the very last moment Martin's bomb-aimer got a sight on both valve-towers. He pressed the bomb release, and the special bomb skipped across the lake towards the dam. The smoke did not seem to hamper the gunners at all, and Martin felt his aircraft shudder as they stitched a row of 20-millimetre cannon shells into his starboard outer fuel tank and ailerons. A streak of fast vaporizing fuel shot out behind the plane, but miraculously it didn't catch fire.

A huge waterspout shot up eight hundred feet into the air behind them as Martin's bomb exploded, but the range must have been slightly misjudged as the base of the spout was not quite centred on the dam. The giant blast wave hurled two of the German gunners from their towers, and they lay senseless on the crown of the dam.

Martin radioed Gibson, "Okay – attack completed."

WHEN THE NEWS of this third unsuccessful attack reached the Bomber Group's headquarters at Grantham, an air of depression gripped the operations room. Barnes Wallis, the special bomb's inventor, buried his head still deeper in his hands so as to avoid the black looks of the two air-marshals pacing up and down.

But the foreman of the Möhne powerhouse, *Meister* Clement Köhler, could see something that none of the British airmen could yet see. Köhler had got out of the powerhouse just in time and was now sheltering beneath a larch-tree halfway up the valley. What he could see was this – fine cracks were forming, branching and spreading along the dam's parapet, and silver jets of water were is-suing from them, glinting in the moonlight. He thought of his six nephews and cousins asleep in their house by the sawmill down the valley – they never paid any atten-tion to air-raid warnings; he thought of the gamekeeper, old Wildening, and the thirty old-age pensioners that he boarded; he thought of the villages of Himmelpforten – "The Gates of Heaven" – and Niederense and the town of Neheim-Hüsten. Nothing could save them now.

BARELY TWO MINUTES after Flight Lieutenant Martin's bombing run, Gibson sent in "Dinghy" Young. "Be careful of the flak," Gibson warned him. "It's pretty hot."

Again Gibson deliberately drew the enemy gunners' fire; he flew his Lancaster up and down the valley on the dry side of the dam with his landing lights blazing, taunting the gunners and firing his guns at them. Micky Martin did the same on the other side.

Young got in his bomb run unhampered while the gunners' backs were turned. Gibson thought that the bomb must have been accurately placed, because the column of water was far taller than after Micky Martin's attack.

Hundreds of tons of water slopped over the crest of the dam, and Young shouted exuberantly, "I think I've done it, I've broken it!" Dave Shannon thought so too: "Christ! that must break the bloody thing!"

As the spray cleared, Gibson saw that the enormous wall of masonry was still intact – but was his imagination playing tricks, or had it bulged slightly since the last two attacks?

With fresh confidence, he called up the fifth aircraft on the radiotelephone, Flight Lieutenant Dave Maltby, and ordered him in to attack.

Maltby's aircraft closed in fast. Two hundred and twenty miles an hour, Wallis had said. His bomb-aimer saw the dam very early, and got good sightings on both valve-towers when still two thousand feet away. The flak defences seemed more subdued. In the centre of the dam, there seemed to be something happening already – Maltby swung his aircraft to port a little. At the precise moment that the towers lined up on the bomb-aimers's two sighting wires he released the bomb.

It bounced three times, smacked into the dam's parapet and settled, still spinning furiously, down the dam's submerged face. At a depth of thirty feet, the hydrostatic fuses detonated the charge – four tons of the most powerful explosive the British had yet devised.

It looked perfect.

The dam was out of Gibson's sight for some minutes as he careered his Lancaster round the valley; his windscreen was still partly obscured by spray. But time was running out. Certain that the fifth attack too had failed, he called up the sixth, Dave Shannon, in AJ–L, and told him to go in.

IN THE MEANTIME, between 12:50 and 12:55 a.m., the Lancasters had radioed to England the coded results of these last three attacks. "Dinghy" Young reported that his weapon had exploded in contact with the dam, Martin radioed that his had exploded fifty yards short, and Flight Lieutenant Maltby believed that his bomb had also failed to breach the Möhne Dam. Guy Gibson signaled the codeword, NO-GO, NO-GO back to England.

HE HAD SIGNALLED too soon. One minute later, Gibson's aircraft thundered over the dam again and as he looked down an awesome, spine-chilling sight met his eyes. The centre of the dam had vanished – it had rolled over. A tidal wave had pushed aside the thousands of tons of masonry and was pounding down the valley. One brave German gunner on the crest of the dam, but only one, was still firing. Gibson swiftly called up Shannon.

"It's gone! It's gone! For Christ's sake, Dave, hold off."

Probably Young and Maltby had between them planted

their bombs in just the right place. Shannon too looked down on the tremendous spectacle moments later, as the whole immense lake began to move. Gathering speed and momentum the water cascaded out of the breach, taking everything in its path like a tsunami. An unstoppable avalanche of mud and water and trees and debris was tearing down the valley.

The Möhne dam had ceased to exist.

"NIGGER was the code word if we broke one," said Shannon fifty years later, recalling the moment as Gibson triumphantly signalled back to Bomber Command. "And after five runs and the loss of one Lancaster over the target, they eventually got their nigger."

FROM HIS SIDE of the valley Clement Köhler had watched, as if paralysed, as the masonry wall had suddenly bulged and then burst with terrible ferocity between the two valve-towers. A mighty wave of water had spilled out of the breach and plunged to the the valley floor, striking the ground with a colossal crash – a sight without parallel in most men's lives. The remains of the power-house vanished in a fraction of a second, and then the tidal wave settled down, the angry vortices and whirlpools vanished, and a wall of water began tearing down the moonlit valley at twenty feet a second, ripping everything with it. Shortly afterwards, a cloud of spray and water-vapour rose, and mercifully obliterated the rest of this infernal spectacle from Köhler's sight.

At four minutes to one a.m., the 'phone rang for the signals officer at Grantham. He listened briefly, then shouted: "Gibson has signalled NIGGER, Sir – they've done it!"

Gibson had already diverted his remaining aircraft to the second main target, the Eder dam. This contained even more water than the Möhne, 202 million tons, making it the biggest artificial reservoir in Europe. This dam was one hundred and thirty-nine feet high, 1,310 feet long, and built of masonry like the Möhne dam.

As Gibson's aircraft reached it, small rivers of water were running out of the dam's overflow channels, so it could not have been more full. The only anti-aircraft guns on this dam had been removed after the defeat at Stalingrad five months before. It was virtually undefended. Only sentries with rifles patrolled the road running along the dam's crest – rifles against the best heavy bomber in RAF Bomber Command.

At 1:32 a.m., the telephone rang in the local Air Raid Defence controller's office. A lieutenant in SS uniform answered: "*Sturmführer* Saahr speaking."

"This is the *Warnzentrale*! There are several enemy aircraft circling the Eder dam!"

An hour earlier, the local authorities in the valley below the Möhne Dam had refused to believe the similar warning telephoned to them by Clement Köhler. But this officer did not hesitate. He shouted to the *Warnzentrale* to clear the line, and at once telephoned the SS unit closest to the Eder Dam, the third Company of 603 Regional Defence Batallion at Hemfurth. The duty corporal there confirmed that there were three enemy aircraft circling overhead.

"I'll call you back in a couple of minutes," said Saahr. "If an attack starts before then, sound the alarm!"

Then Saahr telephoned through to SS *Standartenführer* Burk, the commanding officer of the SS Flak Training Regiment nearby, and warned him that a flood disaster was imminent. Within minutes, the colonel had told one hundred men and trucks to stand by.

Almost at once, *Sturmführer* Saahr telephoned him again, and the news was even more alarming: "The local

"BUTCHER" HARRIS *Air Chief Marshal Sir Arthur Harris, Commander-in-Chief of RAF Bomber Command (top left) watches with Air Vice Marshal the Hon. Ralph Cochrane, No. 5 Bomber Group, as No. 617 Squadron aircrew are debriefed at Scampton airbase*

GUILT-STRICKEN *Dr Barnes Wallis, the boffin who devised the attacks, never forgot the deaths his unusual weapon had caused* battalion says the planes are releasing flares – and they have switched on searchlights!"

The roar of truck engines and motorcycles on the ground mingled with the noise of aircraft engines in the air, as the Germans prepared for the biggest flood-disaster operation in their history.

BELOW THE Möhne dam, the catastrophe was beginning. Clement Mols, the postmaster, had lived all his life in a town downstream from the dam, Wickede. The air raid sirens had suddenly sounded at about eleven-thirty p.m. His wife was already unusually nervous that night. She badgered him to switch on the cable radio and find out where the English planes were.

The news was not good. "Low-flying enemy aircraft above Arnsberg and the Möhne Lake." Arnsberg was close. Mols had sent his wife over to wake their neighbours and then went to the window upstairs – the one with a view up the valley to the lake.

The night was so clear, and visibility good. In the distance he heard aero-engines and a violent detonation, and he distinctly saw a huge column of water shooting up.

For a while after that there was silence.

The cable radio loudspeaker was broadcasting an update. "Low-flying enemy aircraft over the Eder Lake."

There was no more talk of the Möhne Lake. The danger seemed to be past. Clement Mols went down into the neighbours' cellar to tell them – they were mostly women and children, still chattering and joking.

"I think it's all clear," he said. "Back to bed."

His wife was less sure, and urged him to go upstairs again to listen.

As he walked through the post-office he heard the telephone ringing and stopped to answer it. It was the postmaster at Arnsberg: "You're still at the post-office?" the man screamed. "The Möhne Dam has burst, the waters must have reached Vosswinkel by now."

Vosswinkel? That was only three miles away. Dizzy with fear he rushed back next door, yelling. "Get out at once! All of you. Get up to the upper village! The Möhne Dam is broken, the water has already reached Vosswinkel."

At that instant the electric light went out. He shouted to his wife: "You go on ahead! I'll stay here and wake people by phone." She refused to leave.

"Then run over to Mrs Brunberg and wake her up so

she can escape with her three infants, and warn Miss Wilmes too." All their menfolk were away in the army.

Nobody was answering their phone. They all seemed to be asleep. He and his wife took to the hills, literally, making for the upper village – but they had gone only twenty yards when the postmaster suddenly felt the air turn damp. It was like a cold, damp, clammy curtain of fog. "We can't run," he shouted to her. "No time! The water will be here. Back to the house!"

The flood waters overtook them. He slammed the door but the water plunged into the house with colossal force, and a sulphurous vapour cloud came up from the cellar. The batteries in the cellar had short-circuited.

In no time the water rose in the ground floor. He counted the stairs as the level rose, and the first ten were already under water, about six feet deep. It was far deeper in the valley. He looked out of an upstairs window. He could see a freight train a short distance from the railway bridge. The locomotive steam whistle let out a shriek as it drowned in the flood water.

He could see the waters swirling endlessly by, hear cries for help as people struggled to stay afloat in the torrent, and the bellowing of drowning cattle. Beams and planks, prams, furniture, trees, and flotsam rocketed past. Beyond the post-office a truck's trailer floating past like a boat until it tangled on a beam in the yard.

Minutes passed, then hours; the masses of floating debris parading past seemed endless, and still the waters continued to rise. His wife wept and prayed.

"Those were terrible hours," he recalled later. "I tried to comfort her. I pondered on how to get on our neighbours' roof in case the flood swept our house away. Theirs was bigger and had a flat roof. We carried our bedding to the loft. We could not know how high the water was going to rise. I ran from window to window to see how our walls were standing up to the flood waters thundering past. . . And above all this horror shone the beautiful moon, brightly reflected by the water."

IT HAD TAKEN Guy Gibson some time to find the Eder Lake: there was mist in the valleys, and every hollow looked not unlike a reservoir from the air. When he found the right valley he flicked on his microphone and called up the other aircraft: "Can you see the target?"

Dave Shannon's voice came faintly into his earphones: "Can't see anything – I can't find the dam."

It was now well after one a.m., and early summer fog was rising in the valleys. Worse, the lake had several branches. Shannon hurled his Lancaster along the wrong one to start with. There was no doubt. He radioed simply that it was not there. Guy Gibson had his plane right over the Eder dam by this time, and fired a red Verey light, and Shannon's voice came immediately:

"Okay, I'm coming up."

Shannon was an Australian and a perfectionist. At 1:39 a.m., he attempted his first bombing run, but his bomb-aimer was not satisfied and they circled back to the other end of the lake. This was easier said than done: To get out of the valley he had to pull on full throttle and execute a steep climbing turn to avoid a vast rock face. He later used two words from Down Under to describe this exit, carrying a nine thousand pound bomb which was revolving at 500 revs and inflicting its weird gyroscopic forces on the plane from its station in the bomb bay: "Bloody hairy" he called it, and added four more: "to put it mildly."

He tried again, but still the bombing run was not quite right.

Gibson told Dave Shannon to pull out for while and get his bearings, and he sent Henry Maudslay in to attack.

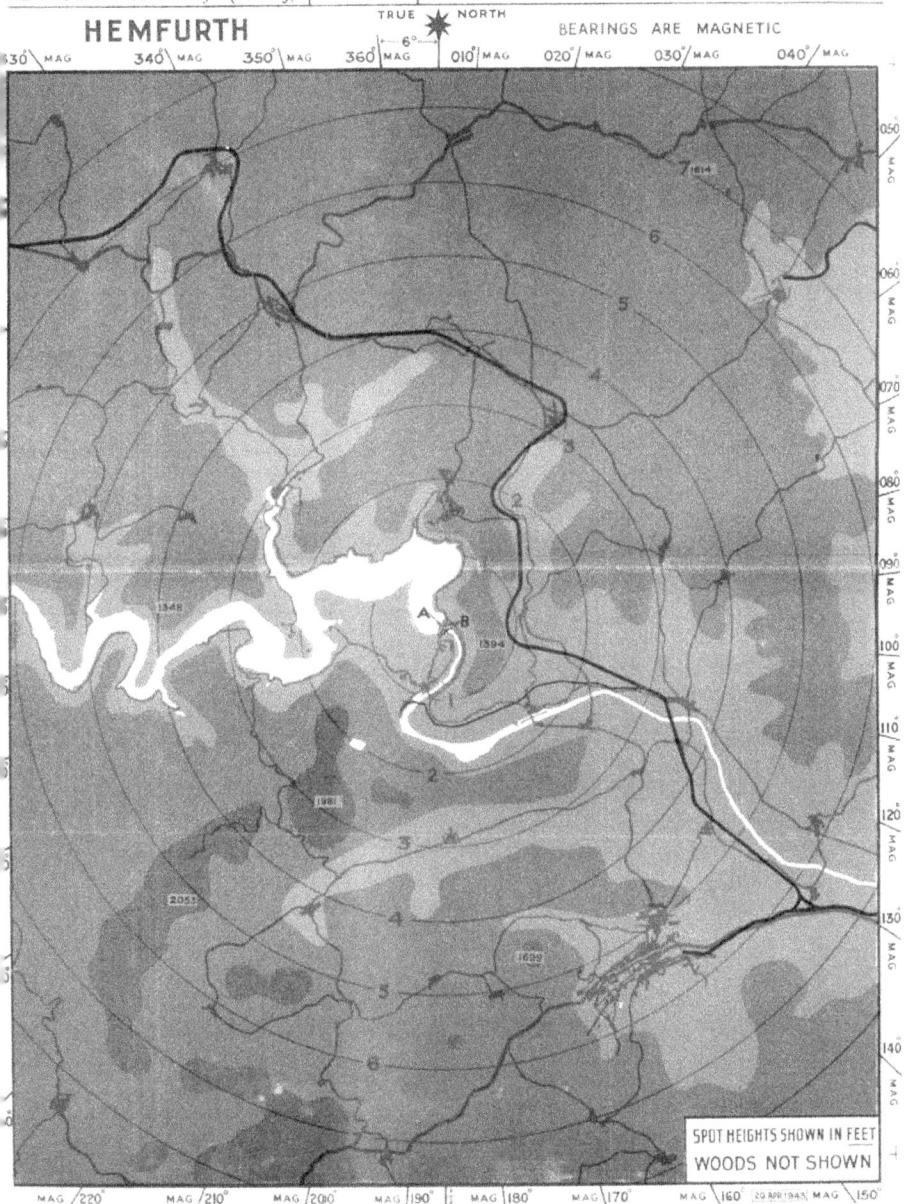

EDER DAM TARGET MAP *In 1943 Bomber Command's maps were printed in black, grey, and magenta, designed for easy viewing in cockpit lighting and comparison with H2S radar images.*

GIBSON CALLED UP the second of the three Lancasters: "Hello Z for Zebra – you can go in now."

It was 1:50 a.m. Squadron-Leader Henry Maudslay dived his Lancaster steeply down over the castle which marked the beginning of the bombing run at the far end of the lake, and closed in towards the dam.

During their bombing trials a few days before, this quiet, athletic English officer had totalled one of these irreplaceable Lancasters when he had dropped the special bomb from so low that the water had damaged the fuselage. There appeared to be no defences on the Eder dam at all, but luck was against him: as Z for Zebra thundered across the moonlit lake, Gibson and his other pilots could see that besides the dambusting bomb, there was some other large object dangling from beneath the plane – it must have been damaged by the enemy defences on the flight out.

Something else must have been wrong, because Maudslay's Lancaster released the spinning bomb far too late from the clutch of its callipers. The bomb volleyed into the Eder Dam's parapet at nearly 250 miles an hour and blew up instantaneously, right beneath the bomber that had just dropped it.

A few of the dam's huge masonry slabs were blown off the parapet like confetti, and a yellow glare lit the whole valley as bright as day for several seconds.

Out of the darkness, somebody's voice on the radiotelephone said quietly what everybody was thinking: "He blew himself up."

Guy Gibson called up Maudslay's aircraft. There was no reply. He tried again: "Z for Zebra, Z for Zebra, are you okay?"

This time, there was a faint, tired reply. "I think so," it said. "Stand by."

But the voice was very weak. Maudslay was dying. His radio operator performed one more duty. At three minutes before two a.m. he sent back to England a coded wireless signal signifying: "Special weapon released, overshot dam, no apparent breach. . . " That was the last that was ever heard of this aircraft or its crew. The lamed bomber crashed with no survivors forty minutes later, finally brought down by light flak near Emmerich.

Gibson ordered Dave Shannon, the perfectionist, back in for his third bombing run against the Eder dam. This time Len Sumpter the bomb-aimer released the special weapon perfectly: it bounced twice, and scored a direct hit on the dam's narrow parapet. Seconds ticked past as the bomb sank, then a mighty explosion rent the air and a pillar of water shot up hundreds of feet into the air, followed by a blinding blue flash as the blast waves short-circuited the 60,000-volt power-lines leading across the valley from the generator house.

As they flew away, Shannon's rear air gunner Pilot Officer J Buckley shouted that there was a bloody great hole below: "Water is pouring out."

But still the dam was standing, and now only one Lancaster remained.

The generator-house foreman, *Meister* Karl Albrecht, later described: "At first we had assumed that the bombers were only using the lake as an assembly point, as they had done so often before. The first bomb fell at about half-past one, but it did not damage the wall much, though it did cause damage to the Power House No. 1. I went to the Power House No. 2, on the right-hand side of the valley by the dam. There were two brilliant flares burning on the little island between the two plants, presumably as an aiming guide for the bombers.

"The aircraft continued to circle . . . "

THE THIRD WAVE of No. 617 Squadron's aircraft was now invading German territory, as an airborne reserve to fill in the gaps. But by two a.m. there were more gaps than aircraft in this reserve: seven minutes earlier, S for Sugar had exploded in mid-air over Tilburg in Holland – the other aircraft could not see why, but German records indicate that it was flying so low that it fouled electric power lines. Its captain, Canadian Pilot Officer L. J. Burpee, had just got married to an English girl, and they had been hunting for a house near Scampton. Now she was already a widow.

In any case, there was already a glow in the East where the dawn was coming up. The last aircraft in Gibson's immediate force, piloted by an Australian, Les Knight, thundered in towards the Eder dam, made one dummy run, and then attacked, using the flares that had been dropped beyond the dam as a rough guide – the flares the generator-house foreman had seen. Guy Gibson, flying alongside Knight and just above him, saw the bomb bounce three times, skip lightly along the lake's surface to the dam wall, sink and detonate perfectly, throwing up an eight-hundred-foot water-spout.

A huge hole suddenly appeared about thirty feet below

the dam's parapet, as though a giant fist had punched through the masonry. Barnes Wallis's special four-ton bomb had started a collapse that would push aside twenty-four thousand tons of masonry.

Gibson ordered his surviving men home. "Get the hell out of it," were the words he used.

There was nothing else they could do. They were out of bombs and did not have enough fuel to reach the Sorpe dam and return to Engand. The second wave of bombers had gone to the Sorpe Dam, but it was an earth-wall dam, and never broken. Barnes Wallis' bouncing bomb was best against masonry.

Dave Shannon did as ordered. He opened the throttles wide and took his Lancaster down as close to the deck as he dared.

He landed back at Scampton at four a.m.; he and his men had been airborne for six and a half hours.

FIVE MINUTES AFTER the dam's collapse, the telephone rang in SS *Standartenführer* Burk's office, waking him out of a fitful sleep. "This is *Sturmführer* Saahr again, Herr Colonel! Arolson Post Office has just phoned through a report from the 603 Regional Defence Batallion. The dam has been destroyed. I have tried to contact them myself, but all the lines are dead."

The villagers closest to the stricken dam needed no telephone. They knew what had happened. A motorcyclist rode through the main street of Affoldern, bellowing at the top of his voice, "The dam's been hit – the water's coming. Everybody out of the cellars!"

Within seconds, the streets were full of scores of people, clutching children and suitcases and scrambling for the higher ground.

There was a noise like a hundred express trains coming down the valley – 8,500 tons of water a second were cascading out of the dam, and the breach was getting wider every moment.

As the people reached the higher ground, they turned round and looked at Affoldern – within minutes it had vanished into the flood. The steel suspension bridge at Hemfurth collapsed with an enormous rumble into the torrent.

The villagers could hear the bellowing of cattle chained and trapped in their stalls, and the screams of those people who had not been able to escape in time.

Standartenführer Burk did not underestimate the size

of the catastrophe. Within minutes, he had telephoned emergency flood warnings to the major city of Kassel, forty miles away, and to the Luftwaffe's big airfield at Fritzlar.

By 2:30 a.m., the Army Command at Kassel had alerted an engineer battalion, and within half-an-hour troops were being rushed by trucks to the disaster area.

At 4:15 a.m., a major emergency was proclaimed. The Royal Air Force had succeeded in doing what the Germans had believed to be impossible, and now the Germans were paying the price.

*

It was at about this time, four in the morning, that "Bomber" Harris, listening to the final signals filtering in to No. 5 Bomber Group headquarters at Grantham, finally said: "Well, that's all we can do here. Let's go over to Scampton and meet them as they come back."

His expression as he turned to the bomb's inventor was softer than it had been earlier that night. "Can I give you a lift, Mr Wallis?" he asked.

Wallis accepted gratefully. Harris's black limousine

was one of the very few yet fitted with a heater – and the early hours in Lincolnshire were chilly.

AFTERWORD: It was the back spin that did the trick

FOR THREE DAYS the local rats disputed Tony Burcher's possession of the culvert. As he lay injured in his hiding place, he thought he could hear a train; he had been told that hopping a freight train was the best hope of getting away from Germany. He was probably delirious. He decided to venture out into the open. He was promptly captured by a Hitler Youth boy patrolling on a push-bike.

"Where the hell did you come from?" asked the boy. He spoke English; most of the better-educated Germans did.

"Up there," said Burcher non-committally.

"What aeroplane were you in?"

"A Tiger Moth," groaned the Australian, anxious to end this interrogation. The boy kicked him for his impertinence, then realised the airman was in a bad way.

Shortly a policeman hove into view, also pushing a bicycle.

They laid Burcher onto some fencing posts strapped between their bikes and wheeled him into the local police station to await medical help.

Burcher asked: "Could I have some water?"

This officer glared at him. "*Wasser*?"

"*Ja*," said Burcher. "*Wasser.*"

The officer fetched another officer. This one spoke English.

"You want water?" he repeated. It appeared that there was none. Burcher suppressed a grin.

"Your people," grunted the German, "have just blown up our supply."

This was the first that the airman knew that their raid had been successful.

THE GERMANS took him to a hospital almost immediately. It was a clearing station for troops injured on the eastern front, and it had skilled doctors. He had thought his back was only sprained, but X-rays showed it was broken. "I received only the best of treatment," he recalled.

Tony Burcher never forgot that he owed his remaining years of life to Hoppy Hopgood and his unselfish act that night. He lived out his life in Hobart, Tasmania, in mounting discomfort from chronic back injuries, and was buried with full military honours in 2001.

*

As dawn fingered the pale May 1943 skies over Lincolnshire, No. 617 Squadron's surviving Lancasters limped back into their home base at Scampton.

An aircraftwoman heard the sound of their engines in the far distance and dashed out with the other WAAFs to the landing strips. "The first planes came in low and taxied to a halt. Then at intervals other planes began to land."

The girls were ordered back to the Sergeants' Mess to start serving the first arrivals. Minutes passed, then an hour; then two. They waited but no aircrew came in.

After two hours their sergeant entered, and called them together: "I must tell you now some very sad news," she began, clearing her throat. "Of our nineteen aircraft, only eleven have returned. Eight have been lost." That meant that fifty-six of those young boys would never come back and mill around these tables again.

"We all burst into tears," recalls the aircraftwoman. "We looked around the Aircrews' Mess. The tables looked empty and pathetic. The sergeant told us to go to our quarters and try to get a few hours sleep. Tomorrow will be another working day."

Of the nineteen No. 617 Squadron Lancasters which had lifted off at Scampton, eight had failed to return – Hopgood, Young, Astell, Maudslay, Byers, Barlow, Ottley, and Burpee. Altogether fifty-three young men "went for a Burton" that night, as Bomber Command's young airmen used to remark with well-feigned indifference in these air force messes in Lincolnshire.

Barnes Wallis listened in horror to their stories. His genius, his invention, had been so costly in young British Empire lives. Dave Shannon said: "He was in tears . . . and a more distressing sight and anguished figure I have never seen to this day."

First the crews that had return had to be debriefed. It took ages. Shaken and still rocky from their long hours in the air, they trooped back to the mess afterwards.They opened the bar, and started to drink – "heavily," said Shannon. Even those who had never touched a drop until now hit the bottle.

"They got well and truly smashed that day. The beer started flowing until late in the morning, when we struggled off to our beds, and managed to get a few hours sleep. Then there was a stand down of seven days for the raid's survivors."

ONLY THREE OF THE missing airmen survived to reach prison camps: Hopgood's bomb-aimer John Fraser and rear-gunner Tony Burcher, and another rear-gunner Fred Tees.

Burcher and Fraser ended up in *Stalag Luft* III, the famous officers' prison camp at Sagan in Lower Silesia. The bomb-aimer told Burcher that he had pulled open his escape hatch as the ground tore past at two hundred miles an hour, only a few feet below the Perspex, and in desperation unfurled his parachute inside the plane. It was again something they had been warned never to do;

after that he remembered only hitting the tail-wheel well as he leapt out out. He landed unscathed and without a mark upon him. In peacetime it would probably have gone down as being the lowest freefall parachute jump in history.

Flight Sergeant Fred Tees was the sole survivor after twenty-millimetre shells from light flak took out an engine of Warner Ottley's Lancaster Mark III, C for Charlie, north of Hamm. He had lost all hydraulic power, and Ottley knew he could not halt the bomber's descent. She was going down out of control. Tees heard him gasp five last words over the intercom just before they hit the ground – "Sorry boys. They got us."

Miraculously the tail was torn off on the first impact. The Germans found Tees alive three miles from the final crash site where his comrades died, but with burns over seventy percent of his body.

After hospital treatment, he was sent to *Stalag Luft* VI at Heydekrug on East Prussia's border with Lithuania. He never really recovered from the trauma of the night; as much still stricken by the death of all his comrades as perplexed by his own survival, he ultimately took his own life nearly forty years later.

OPERATION CHASTISE had been costly on the side of its enemies too, in terms of what is now glibly termed collateral damage. In World War II however it was not collateral, it was intentional. As the tidal waves writhed and crashed down the valleys of the Ruhr, one thousand six hundred and fifty people were killed – most of them, in fact one thousand five hundred and seventy-nine, along the Möhne and Ruhr river valleys; the other seventy-one were killed downriver from the Eder dam. Only about a third of the victims were Germans; no fewer than 1,026 of the victims were foreign workers in a hutted labour camp beneath the Möhne Dam, and of these at least 526 were Russian women captives.

While newsreel cameras whirred, His Majesty King George VI visited Scampton and awarded his country's highest medal for valour, the Victoria Cross, to Wing Commander Guy Penrose Gibson. His comrades won high decorations too, and the men of No. 617 Squadron were fêted for weeks after as national heroes. Air photographs of the raid's devastation gave a fillip to British morale. The squadron went on to even greater acts of heroism and precision bombing, including the "Tallboy" earthquake-bomb attacks on the battleship *Tirpitz* and on railroad viaducts and the V-weapon launch sites and the V–3 supergun site in France.

The destruction of the dams was bound to affect German morale as much as it boosted the British. From the Gestapo surveys, Adolf Hitler learned that there was a creeping resignation among his people, an awareness that the British bombers would always get through. Every night that summer of 1943 "Butcher" Harris was leaving his deadly calling card at some town or other in the Ruhr, as his bombers unloaded thousands tons of explosives into the streets and houses. Soon it would be the turn of Hamburg and Berlin.

SOME DAYS PASSED after the dams raids before Bletchley Park could decode the police signals transmitted by the units rushed into action that night. The Germans, it seemed, had moved with their legendary efficiency to repair the damage. By nine-fifty a.m. on the morning after Gibson's attack the police had already set up an emergency disaster headquarters at Arnsberg, *Einsatzstab* Möhne/Ruhr, the Möhne Operational Headquarters.

The Germans were seized with jitters for weeks after

the dams raid. At 11:55 a.m. on May 20 the British code-breakers monitored a signal from Fröndenberg reporting panic briefly sweeping the Sorpe valley at rumours that the dam there had now been hit. A police company asked the *Einsatzstab*: "Request confirmation whether Sorpe Dam breached. Panic here." Twenty-one minutes later the *Einsatzstab* responded: "Report of dam breach Sorpe false."

Analysts at Bletchley Park concluded that notwithstanding some evidently exaggerated press reports to that effect: "Nothing in any of the material seen suggests public disturbance or rioting on a large scale." The Germans were not a people prone to rioting.

The actual physical effects of the raid were equally disappointing. On June 3 Military Intelligence commented that their "most secret source," as they referred to code-breaking, was finding a disappointing lack of chaos caused by the attacks on dams. Two police battalions, from Cologne and Essen, each numbering four officers and about three hundred men, were trucked into the disaster area with the task of cordoning off areas, redirecting traffic, disposing of corpses, rescuing survivors, and supervising foreign labourers; the deputy chief of police, Major-

General Hans-Dietrich Grünwald came from Berlin to confer with local dignitaries at Neheim-Hüsten.

In fact, the police units had already begun withdrawing four days after the attack, on May 21, and the few Ruhr river bridges which had been closed were reopened to traffic on the twenty-third and twenty-fourth. "It is perhaps also of interest," reported the codebreakers, "to note that up to and including May 23 no message about the dams was reported by the ordinary most secret police source [*i.e.*, decoding], although most air raids have been reflected in requests from German policemen on active service to come home on compassionate leave or, if at home, to have leave extended."

By June 27 the Germans had restored their full water production, thanks to an emergency pumping project inaugurated in 1942, and the generator stations were feeding power at full capacity into the electricity grid. Examined in the harsh light of day, the raids caused only a minor flutter to the heartbeat of the Ruhr armaments industries. Under international law, since 1977 such raids on dams are now deemed to be war crimes anyway.

"Butcher" Harris had meanwhile assigned his bomber squadrons to his more customary bludgeon, the area attacks on cities: upon Churchill's return to England from Washington, where he had been at the time of the attack, Harris called at Chequers, bringing with him the famous Blue Books – bound volumes of maps, pie-charts, histograms, bomb-plots, and damage-photos – pictures by now not just of the flooding resulting from "Operation Chastise," the dams raid, but also of the horrors inflicted on the night of May 29–30 by his 791 bombers in a saturation bombing raid on the Ruhr valley town of Wuppertal-Barmen. It was the first such air raid to kill people in their thousands – over 2,450 civilians died within thirty minutes, most of them burned alive.

Inevitably Mr Churchill saw the other side of the coin too. Now the British had to fear similar attacks on their dams, and on June 7, 1943 he told Professor Lindemann (Lord Cherwell) to report on precautions to protect Britain's reservoirs from similar attacks.

THE DAMAGE TO the dams was repaired in double-quick time, far faster than Barnes Wallis and British Intelligence had estimated. Hitler's munitions minister Albert Speer oversaw an unprecedented effort to rebuild them. Twenty thousand construction workers were drafted in from Holland and France for the task.

While Ministry of Information propaganda officials kept up a drumbeat of propaganda on the heroism and ingenuity of the dams raids, Air Chief Marshal Sir Arthur Harris disparaged the effort – though not of course the men themselves.

Aside from the morale effects, "Chastise" failed to achieve what Barnes Wallis had anticipated, and Harris was privately scathing. As his bombers began a three-month-long and ultimately no more successful attempt to end the war by repeating in Berlin what he had meanwhile done to Hamburg, he wrote in December 1943 to his superiors at the Air Ministry to remind them that he had warned all along against the dams raids:

"For years," he reminded them, "we have been told that the destruction of the Möhne and Eder dams alone would be a vital blow to Germany." But, he continued, "I have seen nothing in the present circumstances or in the Ministry of Economic Warfare reports to show that the effort was worthwhile."

Maintaining a constant battle against what he called such "panacea targets" in his correspondence with Sir Charles Portal, the Chief of the Air Staff, Harris returned to the attack in January 1945: "The destruction of the Möhne and Eder dams was to achieve wonders," Harris complained. "It achieved nothing compared with the effort and the loss." He concluded: "The material damage was negligible compared with one small area attack" – a reference to his saturation bombing raids with incendiaries and heavy "blockbuster" blast bombs.

THE BRITISH air chief marshal's anger was matched however by the fury of the Nazi leaders at this renewed triumph against the Luftwaffe. Their night fighter defences had not scored a single success that night; the losses were all inflicted by anti-aircraft gunfire.

Luftwaffe chief Reichsmarschall Hermann Göring made no secret of his admiration for the brave British airmen: "I have to admit," he told his generals at a Reich air ministry conference, "my respect for those gentlemen grows with every hour... One has to admit, what dash and courage on the one hand, and what contempt for our own fighter defences on the other!"

The next day he heaped mockery on his own feeble bomber forces: "My own men say, 'We are not quite sure whether we will be able to find London in bad weather.'

But the gentlemen on the other side come over and find a dam lying swathed in mist at night, and whack right into it!"

Field Marshal Erhard Milch, his deputy, discussed the one rotating bomb found intact after the raid; it had come from Flight Lieutenant Barlow's Lancaster E for Easy. Milch ordered German industry to copy it, but for some reason they could not get their cloned version to work.

They would not bounce. In fact, they were spinning the bomb the wrong way.

Perhaps the Germans should have learned to play cricket. But then there might never have been a war. It was the back spin that did the trick.

Operation Chastise Aircraft Losses (No. 617 Squadron) May 16–17, 1943

Lancaster III ED887. AJ-A

Squadron Leader H M "Dinghy" Young. Took off 2147 hrs from RAF Scampton and headed for the Möhne Dam and dropped its weapon as briefed. Set course as deputy leader for the Eder Dam before heading for base. Shot down by anti-aircraft fire while clearing the Dutch coast and crashed 0258 hrs off Castricum aan Zee.

Lancaster III ED864. AJ-B

Flight Lieutenant W Astell. Took off 2159 hrs and headed for the Möhne Dam. Crashed 0015 hrs after flying into high voltage power lines near Marbeck, three miles south-south-east of Borken.

Lancaster III ED910. AJ-C

Pilot Officer W H T Ottley. Took off 0009 hrs, briefed to bomb the Lister Dam. Hit by light anti-aircraft fire on outbound leg. Crashed at 0235 hrs on the Boselargerschen Wald near Heessen, two miles north-north-east of Hamm.

Lancaster III ED927. AJ-E

Flight Lieutenant R N G Barlow. Took off 2128 hrs and headed for the Sorpe Dam. Crashed at 2350 hrs after colliding with high voltage power lines at Haldern, 2.5 miles east-north-east of Rees. (The Germans salvaged the "Upkeep" bomb from this aircraft intact).

Lancaster III ED934. AJ-K

Pilot Officer V W Byers. Took off 2130 hrs and headed for the Sorpe Dam. Hit by anti-aircraft fire from batteries on Texel, while flying at three hundred feet outbound, and crashed into the Waddenzee west of Harlingen.

Lancaster III ED925. AJ-M

Flight Lieutenant J V Hopgood. Took off 2139 hrs, briefed to bomb the Möhne Dam. Hit by anti-aircraft fire approaching the target before being crippled by the blast from its own weapon which overshot and exploded beyond the parapet destroying the powerhouse. Crashed at 0034 hrs at Ostonnen, four miles east-south-east of Werl.

Lancaster III ED865. AJ-S

Pilot Officer L J Burpee. Took off 0011 hrs and set course for the Sorpe Dam. Strayed off course and still at very low level, it was hit by anti-aircraft fire and crashed at 0200 hrs near Gilze-Rijen airfield, Holland.

Lancaster III ED937. AJ-Z

Squadron Leader H E Maudslay. Took off 2159 hrs and set course for the Eder Dam. Crippled by the detonation of its own bomb, it was hit by light anti-aircraft fire while trying to return to base, crashing at 0236 hrs at Netterden, two miles east of Emmerich.

Notes and Sources

THE GENESIS OF THIS SHORT book was three chapters written by David Irving for *The Sunday Express*, London, and published in May 1973. They were based on the private diaries and papers of Barnes Wallis, and lengthy interviews with him, and (with H M Government permission) on the papers of Lord Cherwell at Nuffield College, Oxford, and the operational record books of Royal Air Force units including No. 617 Squadron, the "Dambusters."

The author interviewed many officers including Sir Arthur Harris, Marshal of the Royal Air Force, and Air Chief Marshal Sir Ralph Cochrane, AOC-in-C of No. 5 Bomber Group, and participants in the famous raid including Tony Burcher and Mickey Martin. He was also permitted to use Air Ministry files at the

Air Historical Branch, which are now held at the Public Records Office (the PRO, now confusingly rechristened the National Archives). Some research at the German end was conducted by his colleagues of *Neue Illustrierte* of Cologne. The author transferred all his research papers, including copies of relevant pages from the Barnes Wallis Diaries, to the German Federal Archives (Bundesarchiv) but following his arbitrary banning from Germany and specifically from those archives in 1993, the files were returned to him at his insistence and form part of the Irving Collection.

There are many files on Operation Chastise in the Public Records Office including AIR 14/840 (Operation Chastise, Feb–Jun 1943) and AIR 14/844 (Operation Chastise, May 1943). See too the diagrams produced by Wallis to explain how the bouncing bomb "Upkeep" worked: AVIA 53/627. For Guy Gibson see AIR 27/839. For a letter setting out the "dambusting" plan see AIR 14/817.

The codebreaking files are now in the PRO: the quotations on page 123 come from MI14(d)/o/161, a "most secret source" report dated June 3, 1943 (located in a PRO file of "German police reports, unnumbered," file HW 16/9). [There are also three pages of decodes relating to clearing up damage and recovering bodies after the dams raid in HW 16/37, part 2. For the scattered signals intercepted over following days see HW 16/32, part 2: GPD 1496 German Police Decodes No. 1 Traffic on May 18, 1943, decoded on May 21, and GPD 1498 which has a batch of intercepted signals about German sapper (*Pioniere*) operations. The signals about the brief panic resulting from rumours of the breaching of the Sorpe Dam (Page 123) are in German Police Decodes No. 8 Traffic: May 20, 1943, in PRO file HW 16/37 part 2.

Letters between Harris and Portal are quoted from files in the PRO and the Arthur Harris papers archived in the RAF Museum at Hendon. This museum has a good website on the operation, at http://www.rafmuseum.org.uk/online-exhibitions/dambusters

Many papers and personal reminiscences are now available on the Internet and due acknowledgment is made here to this source. Sites include http://dambustersblog.com and http://www.dambusters.org.uk (for example the operational record book of No. 617 Squadron is now reproduced at http://www.dambusters.org.uk/docs/recordbook.pdf). Excellent source material is now also available on http://operation-chastise.co.tv

David Shannon's account quoted on page 41 dates from 1993 – and is now part of an audio collection made for the BBC. See http://www.felixdk.websitetoolbox.com/post?id=2746208

Similarly the WAAF quoted on Page 63 was Aircraftwoman 2nd Class Morfydd Gronland; she was stationed at Scampton at the time. See www.rafmuseum.org.uk/online-exhibitions/dambusters/16_waaf_memoir.cfm

Some of the intercom dialogue on board John V Hopgood's doomed Lancaster Mark III M for Mother, as reported on page 64, comes from letters written by Shannon (pilot of AJ–L) and Tony Burcher (rear gunner in AJ–M, piloted by John Hopgood). See dambustersblog.com/2010/05/27/dams-raid-first-hand-accounts-by-david-shannon-and-tony-burcher

Page 102: Clement Mols was interviewed in October 1945 about the events of May 17, 1943. See http://www.rafmuseum.org.uk/on-line-exhibitions/dambusters

Page 122 collateral damage. Reliable casualty figures have been more recently researched by Ralf Blank: *Die Nacht vom 16. auf den 17. Mai 1943 – "Operation Züchtigung: Die Zerstörung der Möhne-Talsperre*, published by Landschaftsverband Westfalen-Lippe, May 2006. Quoted in http://operation-chastise.co.tv

Page 126 Churchill's warning to Professor Lindemann is referred to in John Martin's minute to Sir Archibald Sinclair and Herbert Morrison, June 7, 1943 (Cherwell papers).

For the reference on Page 125 to International law: Protocol I was added to the Geneva Conventions of August 12, 1949 relating to the Protection of Victims of International Armed Conflicts; dated June 8, 1977, the Protocol I outlawed attacks on dams "if such attack may cause the release of dangerous forces from the works or installations and consequent severe losses among the civilian population"

Göring's remarks are quoted on Page 128 from the verbatim transcript of his war conferences on October 7, 1943, (Milch Documents, vol. 62, pages 5632 *et seq.*) and the next day, October 8, 1943 (*ibid.*, page 5804); see David Irving, *The Rise & Fall of the Luftwaffe* (Weidenfeld, London, 1967) for the rest of the quotations.

A Select Bibliography

Arthur, Max. *Dambusters: A Landmark Oral History*. London: Virgin Books, 2008. ISBN 978-1-905264-33-9.

Brickhill, Paul. *The Dam Busters*. London: Evans Bros., 1951. "Novelised" style. Covers entire wartime story of 617 Squadron.

Churchill, Winston S. *The Second World War*, Volume IV: *The Hinge of Fate*. London: Cassell, 1951.

Cockell, Charles S. "The Science and Scientific Legacy of Operation Chastise." *Interdisciplinary Science Reviews* 27, 2002, pages 278–286.

Falconer, Jonathan. *The Dam Busters Story*. Stroud, Gloucestershire, UK: Sutton Publishing Limited, 2007.

Gibson, Guy. *Enemy Coast Ahead*. London: Pan Books, 1955. Guy Gibson's own account, published posthumously.

McKinstry, Leo: *Lancaster: The Second World War's Greatest Bomber* (John Murray: London, September 2009); and *The Sunday Telegraph*, August 16, 2009.

Sweetman, John. *The Dambusters Raid*. London: Cassell, 1999.

Index

Admiralty, British 18
Affoldern inundated, 113
Air Ministry, British 23, 52
Albrecht, Karl 110
Albright & Wilson 33
Aldis lamps 53
Arolson 113
Astell, Flight Lieutenant William killed 67, 69, 119, 131
Avro company 36; *and see* Roe, A V

back spin 14, 29, 53, 129
Baker, Dr G S: superintendent of the ship tank at Teddington laboratory 24
ball, cricket 15
Barlow, Flight Lieutenant R N G killed 119, 132
Barnes Wallis: *see* Wallis, Sir Barnes Neville
Barratt, Sydney: Sydney Barratt, the chairman of Albright & Wilson 32
battleship, German 13, 18, 69; attacking a 13

Berlin 19, 127
Blackett, Professor Patrick M S: Nobel prize winner, physicist 37
Bletchley Park: GC & CS codebreaking headquarters 123–125
blockbuster, RAF blast bomb 26
bombs: incendiaries 26, 128; bouncing 5, 12, 15, 52, 70, 96, 110; theory of, 12–18, 21, 29, 33, 51, 53, 58, 74; design problems, 36–37, 50–51; German attempt to clone fails 129; diagram of, 12–13, 46, 74; photos of, 40, 46, 88; *and see* spinning bomb
bomber, Mosquito 18; *and see* Lancaster, Wellington, Wellesley
Bomber Command, RAF 26, 27, 34, 38, 72, 98, 100, 101; *and see* Royal Air Force
Brennan, Sergeant Charlie: flight engineer 65, 66

Brown, Captain Harry Albert "Sam" Brown: Avro chief test pilot 44
Buckley, Flying Officer J 110
Bufton, Group Captain Sidney 36
Burcher, Pilot Officer Anthony F 41–2, 55, 57, 62, 64–7, 79– 81, 83– 85, 87, 92, 117–18, 120' bails out, 81–84, 86–87; captured 116–118
Burk, Standartenführer 100, 112
Burpee, Pilot Officer L J 111; killed 110, 119, 133
"Burton," gone for a 119
Byers, Pilot Officer V W 64; killed 119, 132

Castricum crash site at 88, 131
casualties: German, 121–122; RAF 121–122; foreign workers 122
Chadwick, Roy: aircraft designer for Avro 36
"Chastise," Operation 126
Chequers 125
Cherwell, Lord (Professor F E Lindemann): British Government scientist described 19
Chesil Beach 10, 12, 30
Churchill, Winston: prime minister 14, 19; imagination fired 33
Cochrane, The Hon Sir Ralph:

No. 5 Group commander 72, 77; photo of, 101
codebreaking 123–125
Craven, Sir Charles Worthington: chairman and chief executive of Vickers-Armstrong Ltd 10, 11, 31–33
cricket-ball: dynamics of 15, 129

"Dambusters, The": British post-war movie 5
dams, Ruhr 5, 15; damage to, assessed 123–125 *and see* Eder, Möhne, Lister, Sorpe dams
Darmstadt, University of 19
detonator, hydrostatic pressure 36, 96

Eder dam 57, 99–100, attacked 105–06, 108–11, breached 112, 127; photos of 74, 90–91; target map 107
Einsatzstab Möhne/Ruhr 123–24, 140
"Engineer's Way to Win the War, An" 14, 48
explosive, RDX 15, 28, 54, 59,

film demonstrations 10, 11, 18, 22, 25–27, 29, 30
flak: German anti-aircraft guns 57–58, 61, 64–65, 72, 86, 95–96, 109, 121, 131–33
Fraser, Pilot Officer J W 73, 81,

120; photo of 73

Gestapo 123
Gibson, Wing Command Guy
Penrose 35, introduced
38–39; character 41–45,
51–56; brutal and efficient 57,
59–60, 64, 66, 68–71; attacks
Möhne Dam 70–72, 77–78;
draws enemy fire 92–93, 95–
96; 94–99, 105–106, 108–109,
111–112, 122; photos of 39
Gilze-Rijen, Luftwaffe airfield
at 67, 133
Gneisenau, German heavy
cruiser 42
Göring, *Reichsmarschall* Her-
mann, 128
Grantham, No. 5 Group head-
quarters at 72, 94, 99, 114
Green, Flight Lieutenant at Air
Ministry 24
Gregory, Pilot Officer George
H F G killed 65, 66
Grünwald, SS Police Major-
General Hans Dietrich 124

H2S radar 107
Harris, Air Chief Marshal
(later Marshal of the Royal
Air Force) Sir Arthur: commander-in-chief, Bomber
Command 6; hostility of
26–30; reluctance to release
Lancasters 30–31; outraged
33; scepticism 34; 34; 33–35,

72, 77, 101, 114, 125, 127; photos of 101
Hay, Flight Lieutenant R C 43,
92
Hemfurth 100, 113; target map
107
Heydekrug, prison camp at 121
"Highball" 10, 18, 22, 30; *and
see* bouncing bomb, spin-
ning bomb
High Wycombe: RAF Bomber
Command headquarters at
27
Hitler, Adolf: German head of
state 42, 58, 116, 123
Holland 64, 111, 126, 133
Hopgood, Flight Lieutenant
John V "Hoppy" 42; character 61; injured 64–65, 67, 73,
79; heroism of 81, 82–83, 118;
killed 84, 118–120, 132

incendiaries 26, 128
inventors 26, 28

Kassel: flood damage at 114
Kilner, Major Hew Ross: deputy chairman and managing
director of Vickers-Arm-
strong Ltd 18
King George VI, His Majesty
122
Knight, Pilot Officer Leslie G:
attacks Eder Dam success-
fully 111
Köhler, Clement: power sta-

tion foreman, Möhne dam
77–79, 94, 98–100

Lancaster bomber Mark III
22–23, 26, 30, 33, 35–37, 40,
42–45, 48–52, 54–55, 61, 64,
67–69, 77–78, 80, 82–83,
85–87, 95–96, 98, 106, 108,
110, 112, 121
Leggo, Flight Lieutenant J F 43
Lindemann: see Cherwell, Lord
Linnell, Air Marshal F John:
Controller of Research and
Development, Air Ministry
18, 23, 24, 30; opposition
from 33, 35
Lister Dam 132
Lyttelton, Oliver (later Lord
Chandos) 32

Maltby, Flight Lieutenant D H
96, 97, 98
Martin, Flight Lieutenant H
N "Micky" 41, 64; attacks
Möhne Dam 92–95; draws
enemy fire, 95; 97
Maudslay, Squadron Leader
Henry E attacks Eder Dam,
108; blast hits own plane 109;
killed 133
McCarthy, Joe photo 73
Merton, Professor Thomas
Ralph: British physicist and
inventor 14, 32
Milch, Erhard, Field Marshal
129

Minchin, Sergeant John W 82,
83; killed 82, 86
Ministry of Aircraft Production 18, 24, 26
Ministry of Economic Warfare
127
Ministry of Information 126
models 49, 57
Möhne dam 15, 17, 29, 37, 53–
54, 57–59, 68–69; breached
75–76; 77, 86; cracks seen 94,
bulges.96; 97–100, 123, 127;
photos of 17, 40, 75–76
Mols, Clement: witnesses
Möhne flood disaster
102–105
morale, civilian: British 89,
122; German 123
Mosquito bomber 18

National Physical Laboratory,
Teddington 20, 24, 25
Neheim-Hüsten in path of
floods, 78, 92, 95, 124
Nierderense 78
Northolt, RAF airfield 28

Ottley, Pilot Officer W H T
killed, 119, 121, 132

"panacea" targets 127
Portal, Sir Charles, Chief of Air
Staff 25–28, 30; acid cor-
respondence with Harris
34–35, 126
Pound, Admiral Sir Dudley,

First Sea Lord 10–11, 25
Pye, David: Director of Scientific Research, Air Ministry 23

RAAF *see* Royal Australian Air Force
RAF *see* Royal Air Force
Reculver 44, 47, 50, 52, 54
revolving: *see* rotating bomb
Rice, Pilot Officer Geoff 67
Road Research Laboratory 49
Roe Ltd, A V (Avro), Lancaster bomber manufacturer 36
rotating bomb 26, 30, 37, 68, 129; *and see* spinning bomb
Rowe, Norbert Edward Rowe ("Nero"): Director of Technical Development, Air Ministry 35
Royal Air Force Bomber Command:
No. 106 Squadron 41
No. 617 Squadron 39, 41, 49, 51, 55, 61, 86, 101, 111, 118–119, 122
Royal Australian Air Force 41, 43
Royal Society 21

Saahr, *Sturmführer* 100
Sagan, prison camp at 120
Saundby, Air Vice Marshal Sir Robert: Senior Air Staff Officer 27, 29, 34, 38
Scampton: RAF station 41, 55, 60, 67, 72, 86, 101, 111–112, 114, 118–119, 122; photo at 101

Scharnhorst, German heavy cruiser 42
Secret Service (MI6) 74
Shannon, Flight Lieutenant David J 41, 42, 54, 61, 95, 97–98; attacks Eder Dam 106, 108–110,; returns to base 112, 119–120
Sorpe dam 57, 112, 124, 132–133
Spafford, Pilot Officer F M "Spam" 69
Speer, *Reichsminister* Albert 89, 126
spinning bomb 12, 21, 25, 45, 51–52, 60, 96, 108, 129; *and see* bouncing bomb
spotlights, converging: as altimeters 53, 70; *and see* Aldis
Stalag Luft III, prison camp 120
Stalag Luft VI, prison camp 121
steel production 15
Summers, Captain Joseph J "Mutt": Vickers chief test pilot 27, 30, 37, 55
Sumpter, Flight Sergeant Len J 110

tactics 41, 53,57–58, 64
Taerum, Pilot Officer H.T. "Terry" 70; photo of 73
Taylor, Professor Sir Geoffrey Ingram: expert on fluid dynamics and wave theory 48
Teddington, National Physical Laboratory at 20, 24–25

Texel: flak batteries on 132

Tirpitz, German battleship
18–19, 22, 25, 42

Tizard, Sir Henry: British government scientist 20

training 43, 49, 60

Trevor-Roper, Flight Lieutenant R D 43

"Upkeep" bomb 15, 21–22, 26, 30, 33, 36, 43, 88, 132, 143; *and see* bouncing bomb, spinning bomb

Vickers-Armstrong Ltd: British arms manufacturer 10–11, 18, 31–32, 55

Wallis, Sir Barnes Neville: aircraft designer, inventor 7, 9–15, 17–30; threatens to resign, 31–33; relishes a fight 35; says a prayer 36; meets Guy Gibson 37–40; work on special bomb complete 54; briefs crews 58; 40–41, 43–45, 47–63, 65, 67, 69, 71–72, at No. 5 Group Headquarters, 73–76, 94, 113; and 77, 79, 81, 83, 94, 101, 112, 114, 119, 127; photos of 16, 101

water, sulphur-free 15

Wellesley bomber 29

Wellington bomber 10, 11, 22, 29, 55

Weybridge: Vickers-Armstrong works at 10, 37, 55

Wickede: in path of flood 102–105; *and see* Mols

Woolwich, arsenal at 37

Wuppertal, saturation bombing of 126

Young, Squadron Leader H M "Dinghy" 56; successfully attacks Möhne Dam 95–97, 98; killed 119, 131; photo of crashed plane of 88

Zeppelin airship 28

www.ingramcontent.com/pod-product-compliance
Lightning Source LLC
Chambersburg PA
CBHW030526100426
42813CB00001B/164